I0681311

A Clear Horizon

JoEllen Drazan, editor

A Clear Horizon
All Rights Reserved © 2004

Published by Inkblot Books
Dayton Ohio
www.inkblotbooks.com

ISBN 1-932461-06-X

Printed in the United States Of America

A Clear Horizon

Table Of Contents

The Free People of Sedia
JoEllen Drazan

Prologue

Sedia, a city of spiraling towers and glass office build-ings, manicured landscapes and beautiful parks, an artificial world controlled by the organization called Kelo. Hundreds of years ago, after The Great War, Kelo had helped Sedia restore many of the factories and buildings that had been de-stroyed. Piece by piece, the organization had bought Sedia until they owned the entire city. Kelo had become the rulers of Sedia and had created a perfect, almost sterile world for the citizens to live in. The corporation did not allow the citi-zens to leave Sedia, claiming that the outworld had been de-stroyed during the Great War. Beyond the high wall and shield dome surrounding the city was only death and destruction, or so the people had been told. In a few generations, all known knowledge of the lush and beautiful outworld had been for-gotten. Most of the citizens worried little about their way of life, taught to be thankful of Kelo for their generous contribu-tions in creating such a great place for them to live and work.

On the surface it was a perfect place. However, there

were those people on the edge of Sedia who knew differently. Many years ago, rumors spread of citizens disappearing, and creatures roaming the streets at night. Some people started questioning Kelo and demanded protection. The citizens received exactly what they had asked for. The Sedia Enforcement Department (Sed) was created to keep the peace throughout the city and the curfew was instigated. The city was quiet once again. The citizens went about their daily lives, unaware of the true terror residing in their midst.

* * *

Marcus walked down the silent streets of Sedia. Placing his steps carefully, he moved closer to the shadows of the spiraling towers of days long forgotten. He scanned the nearby office complex, nothing moved in the too clean streets between the towering buildings. Hearing the rhythmic footfalls of the Sed Police coming down a side street behind him, he ducked into a shadowed alley between two of city's pristine commercial buildings. Cursing under his breath, Marcus looked down the narrow alleyway to find someplace to hide; even the alleyways were spotless in this forsaken city. Marcus eased his large, muscular frame into a narrow alcove. His dark, utilitarian clothing and long coat helped him blend in to the shadows. The rest of his team had split up to return individually to base.

He had agreed to lead his team on the hunt when one of their informants told them an experiment had escaped containment. They were too dangerous to the group and this one had been found close to the entrance to the underground catacombs where the rebels lived. The energy blasts from their firearms had drawn the Seds around them. He hoped they had escaped.

Most of the experiments were huge creatures, barely

recognizable as men. Uncontrollable monsters artificially bred to destroy. Some, however, were almost human and it was one of these that had killed Stephan, Marcus's brother. His thoughts drifted to the last day he had seen Stephan alive, five years ago.

Stephan had been very eager to introduce Marcus to the new recruit he had found on the streets of Sedia. True to his brother's trusting nature, he had brought one of those things down to the catacombs. Stephan had led the way to the med-dock, telling his brother how fast and how strong this new recruit was, and what a great addition to the team he would be. As a safety precaution, all new recruits were taken to the med-dock to have a through examination to make sure there were no transmittable devices embedded in their bodies. Marcus had smiled at his brother's enthusiasm, but it should have tipped him off right then. The castaways, they usually found on the streets, were half starved urchins who had learned inadvertently about the science program or asked too many questions and had to run for their lives.

They had rounded the corner to the med-dock, both stopping in horror at the scene before them. A garish nightmare of blood and gore had been smeared on the walls and pooling on the floor of the med unit. Stephan's new recruit had been standing over a mutilated body with his back to them. The thing had murdered one of the medical assistants, tearing him to pieces. It turned around. There had been a maniacal gleam in his dark eyes and a snarl had twisted his features to a bestial semblance. Blood had dripped from its mouth as he had rumbled a growl no human could utter. The new recruit had been an experiment. Seeing the beast charge, Marcus had dove out of the way, hoisting his gun out of its holster. Stephan had taken the full force of the beast when it had slammed into him. The beast had torn out his throat before they had even hit the ground. With an angry shout of his own Marcus had emptied his clip into the beast, the flashes from the energy bursts bathing the corridor in an eerie light.

Marcus shook his head to clear his thoughts, *now is not the time to be thinking about the past. Distraction leads to death.* Holding his guns ready, his muscles tensed as the footfalls of the patrol passed the opening of the alley. He let out his breath when the noise faded into the distance. He had not been detected.

Hearing a small gasp behind him, Marcus pivoted around and leveled his guns at a girl. The girl became a blur of motion, and Marcus found himself weaponless, his guns scattered across the pavement. A second kick to the head left him staggering, his dark, shoulder-length hair falling in his face obscuring the view of his opponent. Struggling to maintain consciousness, he forced himself upright and turned to engage the enemy in hand-to-hand combat. Surprise widened his eyes, looking swiftly up and down the alley. The girl had vanished.

Picking up his weapons, Marcus prepared to track the girl, he couldn't let any witnesses know he was in the city. Feeling his position compromised, had no choice but to take her out. Moving from shadow to shadow, he left the center of the city, heading towards the nearby warehouse district.

Marcus scanned the area for any signs of movement. He noticed the girl looking over her shoulder as she entered one of the buildings. She intrigued him. Her head barely came to his shoulder, and at less than half his size, she had disarmed him with practiced ease. Yet, it had been her face that gave her away. The image of her wide-eyed stare had embedded itself in his brain in the fraction of time before her second kick had nearly left him unconscious. She had looked startled that she had known how to react.

Marcus silently entered the building, noticing the security bypassed at the main panel. He crept up the stairs to the upper level where the offices were located. The warehouse was spread out before him. It was packed with pallets that were color-coded and ordered in strict rows, much like Sedia itself. He smiled to himself, just below his position she was walking between the pallets away from him. A movement caught his eye ahead of her. He saw several of the Sed police had entered at the back of the building.

Something about her nagged at the corner of his mind, and a frown creased his brow. She could be the escaped experiment, but he had never heard of the twisted scientists working with female genes. They wanted sub-humans, half beasts who could be used as soldiers, not this slip of a girl. Dismissing the thought from his mind, he marked where the police were stationed and the girl's position. Marcus stole down the staircase and across the warehouse not making a sound. Coming around the last pallet of boxes, he saw the girl looking around the corner of the pallet, facing away from him. Marcus crept forward and wrapped his arms around her, turning her around and holding a hand over her mouth. Fear shown vividly on her face as wide, brown eyes stared back at him. He felt her tense. He didn't trust her not to flee and leaned forward and whispered in her ear, "Seds in back, follow me." Slowly, he removed his hand and held a finger against her lips as he saw she was going to speak. Marcus shook his head and motioned towards the Seds.

He led the way through the maze of cargo pallets to a side door he had spied earlier. It would lead to the alleyway between this building and the next one, which held a gateway they could use to escape. Just as they were on the verge of stepping from the shelter of the pallets, a few Seds positioned themselves in front of their exit. Marcus leaned back against the last pallet and pulled his guns. From what he had experienced earlier, this girl would be able to take care of herself in a fight. Inclining his head to the girl beside him he whispered in a barely audible voice, "Seds ahead. We need to fight to next building, keep close."

Her eyes narrowed with determination, and she gave him a small nod of her head.

Striding out from the shelter of the pallets, he opened fire upon the Seds. Startled by the bright burst of energy from Marcus's blasts, the girl wavered in her initial attack, missing her first target. She rolled onto the floor. Marcus swung around, firing two shots at the Sed standing over the girl. The girl flipped back to her feet and attacked the Sed coming up behind Marcus. Hearing more Seds heading in their direction, Marcus grabbed the girl by the arm and pushed her through the door into the alley.

"Those energy bursts are going to draw half the Seds in the city. We must get out of here now!" Marcus pulled the girl behind him as they raced to the next warehouse.

He stopped in front of the door, quickly tapped the pass code and entered with the girl in tow. He closed the door and set the code to lock it. Punching in a second set of codes, a reinforced metal door slid into place. Marcus turned to the girl. "That won't hold them for long. Listen, I don't know who you are and right now is not the time to find out. I'm going to take you somewhere safe."

Marcus strode ahead, leading the way to the rear of the warehouse. He could hear the Seds blasting at the reinforced door, time was running out. He pulled open a utility door and sent the girl down a set of stairs. Closing the door behind him, he flipped open a hidden panel from the wall and entered another set of codes. He heard the satisfying whir as the field-dampening generator came to life. It prevented the Seds from detecting the energy fields of a gateway. Pressing the panel back into place, it seemed to become part of the wall again.

Marcus joined the girl at the bottom of the stairs, opened the communicator and called into it urgently, "Base! We need a gateway now! Warehouse eight, two bio-stamps." Marcus held out the communicator in front of him and placed his hand over the device as the screen flashed red.

"Bio-stamp one, matched," a female metallic voice responded. Marcus grabbed the girl's hand and placed it over the screen as it flashed red once more. "Bio-stamp two, no match. Request authorization."

"Authorization: Marcus Omega-8-5-9," Marcus intoned, wincing as he heard the explosion as the outer door was breached.

"Authorization accepted," the feminine voice replied.

"Step back." Marcus tugged on the girls arm, bringing her to stand with him against the far wall. "A portal will open. When I go, you go with me. Don't struggle, we will only have one chance to enter it together." Marcus looked up the stairwell as he heard blasts against the door. "Damn, I hope there's enough time."

A soft bluish light appeared in the center of the floor. Gathering in strength and brightness, swirling together, it coalesced in to a circular area. Static electricity flashed around the edges. The gateway opened and a rush of wind surrounded the two people. They could see a black void in the middle of the light.

Just as Marcus pulled the girl to him to enter the gateway, the door to the stairwell burst open. The Seds passed through the splintered door, their boots thudding down the stairs. Marcus gathered the girl into his arms and leaped into the gateway as shots whizzed overhead when the Seds opened fire. Bone numbing cold embraced his body as he held the trembling girl. Traveling the gateways was unnerving even for the seasoned veteran. He gave her credit, she did not scream. A heartbeat later, they emerged over a padded dais. Careful of the girl as he landed, he rolled with her away from the gateway's electrical charge.

Marcus let go of the girl and rose to his feet, speaking into the communicator, "Base! Two received. Cut the gateway, disable for future use, position compromised." The gateway shut down with a resounding clap of thunder.

"Position compromised. Fuck. What happened out there Marcus? Your team was back an hour ago. Who the hell it this?" a gravelly voice said from behind them. A burly man waited with a long blaster aimed at the girl. His wizened face and white hair belied the cold intelligence in his sharp blue eyes and strength in his broad shoulders. He wore the same dark utilitarian clothing as Marcus, clearly a military man.

"Actually Russ," Marcus said, turning to help the girl up. "I have no idea who this young lady is or why the Seds were chasing her."

"The Seds? You were damn lucky you didn't get caught yourself," Russ kept his gun leveled at her. "You know the rules, hell you made half of them. She needs to go to Meddock to get checked out."

Marcus ignored the command for a moment, "What's your name, girl?"

The girl looked hesitantly at Marcus, glancing sideways

to the gun Russ was holding on her, "I-I'm not sure. I mean, I don't know. I don't remember." She hung her head. Her long brown hair fell, hiding her face as she wrapped her arms around her middle.

Marcus looked at Russ and raised an eyebrow.

* * *

"Marcus, come here a moment." The head of the med-dock team propped open the door to the common room. "I need to speak with you about our new guest."

"What's the matter, Jonas?" Marcus placed his morning coffee on the table in front of him.

"Come with me, I have a few things to go over with you, and it is best done on the way to the med-dock," Jonas said, waiting for Marcus to join him.

"So what's wrong with her?" Marcus asked, walking with Jonas down the corridors.

"She's bugged," Jonas stated, his mouth pressed in a firm line.

"Damn," Marcus swore, trying to figure out a way to deal with this mess without actually killing her, "and her memory loss?"

"That is the most curious thing of all, Marcus. She cannot tell us anything about who she is, or why she was running. I haven't told the other team members, but there's something else I discovered." He looked over to Marcus. "She's not entirely human."

"What do you mean?" Marcus followed Jonas to the shielded area of med-dock.

"She doesn't have the experimented genes we usually see. Her genetic makeup is something else entirely, but still nearly human." Jonas keyed into the security panel and pushed open the metal plated door to the med-dock. "To put it simply, humans have a set pattern of genes, she has all of the human genes and some more that are not," Jonas said, and more to himself, he finished, "I don't know what those other genes are for. I've never encountered anything like it."

Marcus followed Jonas through the second set of doors to the holding area for new arrivals. His brows furrowed into a thoughtful frown, he reached out to stop Jonas, "So what is it that you are not telling me. Will she need to be," Marcus's voice turned grim, "terminated, or not?"

Jonas turned to his long-time friend, "I can't answer that question just yet. She is nothing like we ever have encountered. The bug I mentioned is also unique. It is a neuro-transmitter of unknown manufacturing. I have never seen such intricacy in a medical application. It's implanted at the base of her skull."

"Utterly fascinating," Marcus interrupted him, never really understanding all the scientific things that Jonas thrived on, "but I need to know if she is a danger to us. Does that bug transmit signals to the surface? Can you remove it?"

Jonas sighed, putting his hands in the pocket of his lab coat, "Yes, I believe it can be removed safely. However, I would like to run a few more tests before we proceed. I did a frequency scan and it does produce a small signal, but our shielding is blocking it."

"I figured as much," Marcus said. "It is probably how the Seds were tracking her. You have until this afternoon to complete the surgery. Where's the girl? I'll tell her myself, if you haven't already done so."

"This way," Jonas said, turning to lead the way to the holding room assigned to the girl. Unlocking the door to the sparsely furnished medical room, he stepped aside to let Marcus enter. "I'll be waiting in my office, just buzz the com when you're through," Jonas said, pulling the door shut as he left them alone.

The girl was sitting on the narrow cot, her knees drawn up with her chin resting on them, looking up at Marcus, and silently regarding him.

"Hello," Marcus begun awkwardly. "There are a few things I need to tell you about what Jonas found. First, I can't keep calling you 'girl'. Have you picked out a name?"

"Yes, Jonas helped me pick one out," she said eagerly. "My name is Emily."

"Emily." Marcus smiled at her. He pulled a small chair over to the bed and sat down in front of her. "There is no other way to say this, so I'll just come out with it. Jonas has found a transmitter embedded within your body. This may be the reason that you have no memories."

"What's going to happen to me?" Emily asked, looking up at him.

"Jonas wants to surgically remove the device today. After that, you will stay here until you recover from surgery. Then we will see if you can remember anything," Marcus answered.

"And after that?" she questioned as a small frown appeared on her brow. "What if I still don't remember?"

"I can't answer that right now," Marcus said softly, looking down at her sadly.

* * *

Marcus sat in a chair outside the operating wing of the med-dock. He wasn't looking at the daily reports from his men that he had in his hand for the past hour. His thoughts were on the girl on the operating table behind the steel doors. He was startled out of his thoughts, when the doors swung open and Jonas walked up to him.

"It's done. The transmitter device has been removed and put in a shielded container for study later," Jonas informed him.

"And the girl?" he asked.

"The girl will be fine. She'll wake up in a couple hours. Come on, I could use some coffee and I'll fill you in on the details." Jonas scrubbed a hand through his hair and walked off in the direction of his office.

Left with no choice, Marcus followed. He sat down on the chair across from Jonas's desk. Leaning back, he crossed his arms waiting for Jonas to continue his explanations. What he heard, through all the scientific babble, was that the girl would be trouble.

* * *

"I'm here for the girl, she's to be moved to her own quarters." Russ informed Jonas, striding into his office.

"Marcus didn't mention anything to me," Jonas replied, taking off his spectacles with a frown.

"Believe me, I'd rather be anywhere else than babysitting the little brat, but I have my orders. I want to get this done, and I have patrol duty this afternoon." Russ said, impatiently shifting his rifle. As usual, it was not holstered.

"Sure, right this way." Jonas led Russ to the girl's holding room, "Where are her new quarters? I'll want to check on her tomorrow to make sure she hasn't opened the stitches from moving around to much."

"She'll be put with the rest of the people in the lower caverns," Russ grunted, trying to hurry Jonas along.

Jonas gave Russ a sidelong glance, knocking on Emily's door, "Emily? You have a visitor."

"Come in," came the faint reply.

Jonas opened the door and stepped aside to let Russ

through. "Russ is here to show you to your new living quarters."

Russ looked around the sparse medical room. Its white decor always gave him chills. Spying the standard issue personal chest, he asked, "Are you ready to go girl? Everything is in that chest, right?"

"I thought Marcus was coming for me later," Emily said, a small frown of confusion lining her brow.

"Marcus is on patrol duty until late this afternoon, he sent me to get you resettled." Russ walked into the room. He slung his rifle over his shoulder into the holster strapped across his back and reached down to pick up her chest. "Get whatever else you need and follow me."

Russ led Emily down through the lower caverns. Most of the inhabitants were not present at this time of day as they were off to work sections. The few that they passed paid them no heed. It was not uncommon for Russ to be walking about the lower caverns any time day or night to access the tunnels to the upper city.

He walked past the busy common sections to the private residences. He kept an eye on the girl beside him, not trusting her not to go off on her own. Spying the unoccupied residence, he ducked inside and placed her chest on the floor. He turned to face her and retrieved his rifle. He was rewarded by her shocked and fearful expression.

"We are going for a little walk." Russ motioned towards the door. "If you try anything, I will kill you."

"Where are we going?" Emily asked, backing away from him and into the walkway.

"You'll find out when we get there. Now, go left," he commanded.

Russ followed her waif-like form towards the entrance

to the back tunnel. Opening the wheel-locked door, he pushed her through and swung the heavy door shut behind him. Pale overhead lights illuminated an old, abandoned mining tunnel. Pieces of rail and rotted wood could be seen jutting from the uneven floor. Rocks of various sizes were strewn across the floor from cave-ins. To the left there was a small alcove set with chairs and monitors. He had made sure that the schedule had left the post unattended for the hour.

The post itself was hardly needed on this side of the catacombs, none of the tunnels led towards the city. Long ago, his people had mapped this tunnel for a full day until they came upon an impassible cave-in. Still, in the measure of security for his people, he never left any tunnel entrance unattended. Keeping the rifle leveled at her, he shouldered a pack that he had placed there earlier and grabbed a coil of rope.

Once they were far enough away, the base's detection systems would not register the discharge of his weapon. He would make sure that he would be the only one to return. When Marcus's father died, he had sworn an oath that he would take care of his children. He had failed once, but today he would keep that oath and make sure Marcus would be safe from this experiment. A grim half-smile twisted his features as he followed the girl deep into the tunnels.

* * *

Marcus returned from an uneventful patrol duty of the western slides. After cleaning up, he went down to the Meddock to see if Emily was ready to go. Walking up to Jonas, he saw a puzzled look on his friend's face.

"What are you doing here, Marcus? I thought you would be spending time with Emily getting her settled." Jonas put down the cup of coffee he was holding.

"Well, that is why I'm here," Marcus replied, feeling confused. "Is she ready to go?"

"Russ already came and got her hours ago. He said that you told him to get her settled in her new residence in the lower caverns." A frown crossed Jonas's face. "You didn't send him, did you." It was not a question.

"No, I did not." Marcus ran a hand through his hair in frustration. "Shit. How long ago did they leave, exactly?"

"Five hours."

Marcus rushed out of the Med-dock, his long strides carried him swiftly down the corridor and out to the lower caverns. He hoped his long-time friend had not lost all sense of reason, and he worried that he would not be in time to prevent Russ from doing anything stupid. Stopping briefly at the duty station, he checked the logs for any time that Russ had made available for him to move freely out of the complex with the girl. Seeing the gap in the schedule for the back tunnel, Marcus knew where Russ had taken her. Snapping the binder closed, he grabbed one of the light duty packs they always wore when out on patrol. It was filled with the assorted rations and implements that were needed if a person were to be unable to return to the caverns by nightfall. Wasting no more time, he started his pursuit.

He spent the long hours pacing himself at a trot-walk down the tunnel, following two sets of prints in the dirt floor. His mind raced with scenarios of what he would see when he found them. Each scenario became more gruesome and more heart wrenching as time wore on.

Unable to continue, he was forced to stop for a brief rest. Sitting down against the cool rock wall, he pulled out the duty pack and withdrew one of the ration bars. Leaning his head back against the rock wall, he closed his eyes against the harsh overhead light.

Why Russ? he asked himself, but he already knew the answer. *Russ had always thought the girl was an experiment. Hell, he thought everyone we brought down from the surface was an experiment.*

Russ was smart enough to not risk alerting the base to an energy discharge from his firearm. It would take him at least twelve hours to get out of range of the sensors. Marcus hoped to find them before time ran out.

* * *

Emily walked ahead of Russ, trying to think of a way out of her predicament. She would have to catch him by surprise, or risk being killed by the rifle he held at her back. They had rested only briefly throughout the night. The lack of sleep and exertion from the fast pace Russ set was taking its toll on her already tired body.

The last few days were all she remembered, but she still felt unnaturally lethargic from the drugs present in her system. Just yesterday, Jonas had identified one of the drugs as a compound depressant. He had assured her that the drugs would leave her system naturally. It seemed a much longer time had passed since they had entered the tunnels. She wondered briefly if Marcus was trying to look for her. Pulling together her scattered thoughts, she decided that she couldn't wait for him any longer.

"Why are you doing this?" she asked, trying to get Russ to break his stony silence.

"To protect Marcus and my people," Russ replied, using his rifle to nudge her to move faster.

"To protect him from me? What have I done?" She couldn't believe that Russ thought that she was a threat.

"As if you don't know. I see through your lies. You are an experiment and you will go back to them and tell them all about us, the rebels. You will be our destruction and Marcus is to young and trusting to realize it," Russ said with a surety that chilled her blood.

"What are you going to do to me?" she questioned, fearing the answer.

"Make sure you won't trouble us again. Now, shut up and keep moving." He pushed her roughly.

Emily realized that she was dealing with someone who was completely insane. For many minutes, she searched the rubble strewn across the floor for a weapon of any kind. Spying a piece of loose railing on the floor just ahead, she pretended to stumble and fell to the floor hiding the metal under her body.

Lying still, she waited until she felt Russ' hand on her shoulder. Rolling over quickly, she kicked his rifle out of his hands and placed another kick to his chest causing him to stager back. Flipping to her feet, she held the piece of twisted rusted metal in her hands. Not giving him a chance to recover, she pressed her advantage and attacked again.

Russ was not easily caught off guard and recovered more quickly than she anticipated. He grabbed the metal on her down stroke and pulled her closer, delivering a heavy punch to her ribs. Pain blossomed in her side as she felt one of her ribs crack. She elbowed him in the chest and twisted away, leaving the piece of metal in his hands.

Throwing the metal aside, Russ advance on her. His many years of military training showed in the way he moved with cool precise steps and a grace that a cat would be proud of. Keeping her right arm over her injured side, she looked at her opponent trying to find an opening to attack.

Russ didn't give her a chance to attack. He closed the distance between them and slammed his fist into her jaw.

Falling to her knees, she spit blood. Before descending into unconsciousness, her last thought was of Marcus, and her hope that he would find her.

* * *

Marcus spent the night pursuing them. The brief times he had stopped to rest, the images of her dead body always had spurred him to his feet. Russ had raised him and his brother after their father died. Marcus knew that Russ was a soldier first and took whatever means necessary to keep the catacombs safe, including killing. This time Russ was wrong.

He stopped when he noticed signs of the scuffle. Kneeling down, he placed his hand on a dark stain in the sand. Grasping the moist sand in his fist, one thought went through his mind, *Blood, her blood.* It was still fresh.

A sharp scraping sound echoed from down the corridor, bringing Marcus to his feet, listening for more sounds. He heard a man talking almost mumbling. He could not make out the words but he was sure it was Russ's gravely voice. Silently, he moved down the tunnel, keeping close to the wall.

Leaning his back against the wall where the tunnel curved, Marcus lifted his guns. Hearing the powering up of a rifle, Marcus thought he was too late. Charging around the corner, Russ and the girl came into view.

"Stop!" he shouted, leveling his guns at Russ. Emily was bound and gagged facing the tunnel wall with her back to them. He could see she was visibly shaken and bruised. "Let her go."

"Fuck!" came the reply. "What the hell are you doing here Marcus?" Russ swore, not taking his rifle off of her. "She has tricked you into helping her and having her alive is a danger to us. She knows about us now, and she will report back to them." Russ readied his blaster, "If this is hard on you lad, then I suggest you back off. I'm fulfilling my promise to your father to keep you safe. I failed your brother, but I won't fail you."

"Russ! Don't make me do this. You have known me all my life. If she was one of those creatures, you know that I would have more reason to hate her than anyone," Marcus pleaded to his life long friend. He saw Russ reach for the trigger.

"No!" Marcus shouted, getting Russ's attention once again, "You must trust my judgment! For once in your life I am not the little boy you are sworn to protect. I haven't been for a long time. Lower your weapon Russ, I'm not asking you. I'm telling you." Marcus charged his gun for the first shot.

Russ looked over his shoulder at Marcus, "You would chose her over me, someone you have considered family?"

"I would rather not chose at all," Marcus replied with sad determination. "But you leave me little choice. She is not one of them."

"Lower your weapons, both of you," interrupted a voice from the darkness beyond the overhead mining lights.

Marcus swung his guns towards the sound. "Who are you? Come forward and reveal yourself."

"Very well," came the reply. A tall figure stepped into the glow of the overhead lights and reached up to draw back his hood. Dark, almond-shaped eyes looked out from youthful features, high cheekbones accentuated his narrow face, and ears pierced with multiple, small, ornate hoops could be seen from his curtain of silver hair. On the left side of his face, strange markings seemed to shimmer against his pale skin. Dark bands of coal crossed his sand colored cloak and with what looked like a strange form of writing sewn into the band bordering it. His black uniform was made from a fabric never seen before in Sedia. It seemed to absorb the light and shift in different shades as the stranger walked toward them.

"Answer. Who the hell are you?" Russ commanded, still keeping his blaster on the girl.

"I am Garvin, from a city far outside your walls. The girl is my daughter, stolen from me over a year ago."

"You barely look any older than she does," Marcus said in disbelief, his gun raised a little more reading to fire. "You lie, now state your true purpose," he demanded.

Garvin raised his hand in front of him and conjured a sphere of pale light in his palm. Holding his other hand toward them, he spoke softly with an assuredness that was not quite a threat, "Weapons are no use against me. Those who follow my order are protected. We wield a power as ancient as time itself and as sacred. I have come for my daughter."

"Fuck, this just gets weirder every second," Russ swore.

Marcus looked over at Russ for guidance, "Well, what should we do?"

Russ chuckled, the tense situation defused for the moment. Removing his hand from the trigger he allowed his rifle to charge down. "Seems to me there's nothing that has been normal since you brought this girl down with you." He motioned to the stranger to sit next to the girl. "Lad, I don't know about you, but lets hear this out. You can decide whether or not to shoot me later."

Holstering his guns, Marcus went over to Emily and started untying her bonds. "What the hell did you do to her?" He looked at Russ angrily.

"She turned to fight me, and I knocked her out," Russ replied with a grunt as he sat down on a boulder across from them.

"I'll be ok, but I think my rib is cracked," Emily grabbed Marcus's hand, stopping him from checking her for other injuries.

Marcus stripped off his shirt and tore it into lengths to wrap around her ribs securely. "It'll keep you stable until we get you to Jonas."

"Who is this Jonas?" the stranger asked, watching the interchange between them.

"Before you tell him anything, Marcus, I want to know more about him." Russ stated, shifting his rifle to a better position.

Marcus looked at Russ, still not trusting him to not open fire on the stranger or Emily. He finished tending to Emily's injury and sat next to her looking at the stranger expectantly.

"Well, yes, I do believe that I can give you more information. We are hardly a secret outside your city. 400 years ago, after the Great War, the organization Kelo, took over and shut your city from the outside world. All the non-humans were exiled, left to roam as they chose as long as they did not come close to the city walls. Once the dome was built, few even tried. Those that did have not returned." Garvin paused and drew a flask out of a pouch at his waist and took a drink. "We believe that long ago the government of your city created the desert to remove itself further from the rest of the world. There are other human cities beyond the desert, and some are quite prosperous."

"Lies," Russ declared. "I've been outside the dome many years ago. There is nothing but sand as far as the eye can see. There are no living things out there."

"Then were did I come from?" the stranger asked him with a small smile. "Things are not always what the seem, beyond the sands there is a lush world of plants and animals and many races. You mentioned I look young. My race lives just over twice you humans do. I am still young for my race."

"So you are here to get Emily and go back to where ever it is you come from?" Marcus asked. He knew he was missing something here. Garvin seemed too formal to just be searching for a daughter he lost a year ago.

"Emily?" Surprised, Garvin looked over at his daughter. "Do you not remember your name?"

"No," Emily began, "I believe I was captured and held for some kind of experimentation. Marcus helped me escape from them a few days ago."

"And him?" Garvin nodded his head toward Russ.

"He thought that Emily was one of the experiments we had encountered before. Those experiments that we know to be genetic alterations of Sedia's citizens. The Kelo's scientists are trying to create the ultimate soldier, for what purpose I do not know. Sedia was designed to be a peaceful city. My father had learned of the experiments when he had worked for their labs. When he had questioned his superiors, they had turned on him and we had to run for our very lives. Russ took my father, brother and myself down here to the catacombs twenty years ago to join the rest of the rebels," Marcus explained. "Russ had thought that Emily was a new version of those experiments, and had acted to protect us."

"Emily's real name is Vara and she is of my kind." Garvin took one of Vara's hands. Frowning thoughtfully, he spoke in a softer tone, "her magic seems to be inhibited by something. Do you know if anything else has been done to her?" He directed the final question to Marcus.

"When she arrived at our Med-dock, she had a neuro-transmitter embedded at the base of her skull. It was removed three days ago. Our medic also found trace foreign substances in her blood but was not able to figure out what they were for. He assumed that her body would flush them in time." Marcus leaned back against the tunnel wall and allowed Vara to lean against him resting her head against his shoulder.

"How many more of your kind is there?" Russ inquired.

"Well, about two hundred thousand of us live in a city to the north of here. Though, many of us prefer to travel across the lands. It was at one of the camps that the people from your city raided and took Vara. It was the first raid of many that occurred over the course of several months. Over twenty of our people have been taken."

"Why did it take you so long to come after them?" Marcus's thoughts were churning, *maybe this was the ally they needed to infiltrate the science labs and stop the madness once and for all.*

"We did not know that Vara was here until just a few days ago. Apparently when your medic removed that device from her brain she was able to contact us on a subconscious level." A smile broke across his face, "Once I felt her mind try to reach us, I came here immediately. I would assume the others also have these devices implanted in them, which would be the reason I cannot detect them."

"Wait a minute," Russ interrupted them. "There is no exit to this tunnel system except one, and I know you did not come through that way. How the hell did you get down here?"

"Like this," he said simply. His form shimmered before them and disappeared.

Marcus looked at Russ whose eyes were just as wide as his must have been. "That's impossible."

"Not impossible," Garvin said, walking around the corner of the tunnel. "It is a little more difficult to phase in and out of a small location such as these tunnels, one slip and I could end up encased in the stone itself."

"Now that you are here and Vara is safe, what are your plans?" Marcus asked.

"My plans? To find the rest of my kind and get them back," he stated.

"It's going to take more than you to get past the security in Sedia. We've been trying for fifty years to infiltrate their system, not possible." Russ said.

"The securities to any facility have never been a problem for us to phase through." Garvin paused for a moment, "There are several more of us on the surface just outside the city waiting for me to return. If we join forces, then perhaps, we have a chance of getting our loved ones back."

With grim hope, Marcus turned to Russ, he still ranked over him in the militia and it was his decision for the fate of the rebels.

Russ remained silent as he came to his decision, and then he spoke slowly as if the words were forced from him, "Call them." He returned Marcus's stare. "This may be the only chance we'll ever get of getting rid of Kelo."

* * *

"Are you sure you are strong enough for this?" Marcus asked, walking beside Vara down the exit tunnel they would use to get close to Kelo's science building.

"Yes," She replied firmly. "Stop worrying over me, even Jonas said I was fit to go." Vara shifted her pack over the cloak her father had given her. She had recovered her memory only a week ago, waking up in the small hours of the morning, screaming from nightmarish memories.

Marcus gave her a small encouraging smile. These past three weeks have been the most interesting of his life. Garvin's several people had turned out to be several hundred people and all of them possessed the same strange and powerful magic. Many of them, at one point or another, had revealed to them the more deadly aspect of their powers. Marcus was glad that they were on his side.

The lower caverns were now evacuated. The women with children and some of the men would wait in the rear tunnels for word to flee with Garvin's people to the outside world. Hopefully, if things went well, they would join them.

Marcus stopped at the tunnel's exit and turned to the assembly that stretched far back through the tunnel. The faces of the men and women looked back at him solemnly, ready for what lie ahead. Each one of his people was paired with one of Garvin's people for best tactical advantage while in the building and if anything went wrong the magic folk could phase his people out of the buildings. He pumped a fist in the air in salute and turned to open the hatch to the street that would lead directly to the science complex.

Swiftly, the men and women scattered into the night, disappearing into the shadows. Many of them had worked in Kelo's science buildings at an earlier point in their lives. When they had questioned their superiors about a few things they saw, they had found themselves on the run for their lives, much like Marcus's father. These people were the key to infiltrating the buildings.

Marcus followed Russ to the back of one of the three buildings that made up Kelo's science complex. Russ had worked here with Marcus's father many years before, and he knew where the experimental chambers were located. Garvin and Vara followed close behind.

"Right behind this wall is an open shipping area we should be able to phase through to clear space," Russ grimaced. He had made his protestations clear about using magic to enter the complex. In the end, he had agreed reluctantly that it was the best offensive move.

"Be ready to move once the power is cut." Marcus grabbed hold of Vara's hand and readied himself for the vertigo that he would feel once they phased through the wall.

Garvin placed his hand on Russ's arm. "We will need to move fast once inside. I expect they will have back up energy sources, but I do not want to take more chances with my people than necessary."

"We'll get them out, Garvin," Marcus assured him. Darkness descended upon them, when the first group had successfully cut the main power.

"GO!" Russ urged, taking the first step toward the wall before he and Garvin vanished.

"Ready?" Vara looked at Marcus. Squeezing his hand, she phased them inside the building.

Marcus felt the world tilt, and his body turned numb. Once he was in the building, he stumbled as gravity once again took hold of his body. He leaned over, trying to gain his bearings and took deep breaths. He had insisted he and his men practiced phasing to get used to the feeling. Still, it was not pleasant.

Sirens sounded throughout the building, and the emergency lights came on. Russ was standing by one of the doors with his charged rifle slung low.

"Let's go," Marcus said, walking through the door and started down the metal stairs. The others followed, trying to make as little noise as possible. Kelo, in its arrogance, had little in the way of security other than personnel. The corporation had never expected a handful of rebels to be able to attack them directly.

They arrived at the lowest level when a blast was heard from above and they felt the tremors from the percussion of several more. Marcus looked at Garvin with a raised eyebrow, thankful once again that the energy they controlled was used on their side.

"This way is the control room for the chambers," Russ said, his gravely voice barely above a whisper. "There will be guards once we go through the first set of doors. Marcus and Vara, you two will go down to the lab at the end of the hall while I disable the controls with Garvin standing guard."

Russ blasted the shielded doors repeatedly before they came apart, flying off their hinges in a protesting screech of metal. The blasts had allowed enough time for their enemy to gather in the hallway. More than a dozen men with weapons drawn faced the four of them. Russ and Marcus dove to the side, returning lethal fire. Garvin and Vara stood in front of the security guards with their hands spread before them, creating a charged shield around themselves and protecting them from the energy bursts of the weapons.

The guards fired most of their shots at the two mysterious strangers. Marcus and Russ used the twisted doors as shields and took out the guards, clearing the hall in few minutes. Blinking away the haze left by the weapons' energy discharges, they moved into position near the control room doors, stepping over the bloodied bodies.

At a nod from Russ, Marcus and Vara continued down the hallway to the last set of doors marked LAB – AUTHORIZED PERSONEL ONLY. At the sound of Russ blasting the doors to the control room, Vara lofted a ball of yellow energy towards the lab doors. When it touched the doors, the energy spread over them seemingly to soak into the metal. With a solid kick, the doors shattered as if made of glass.

Vara led the way through the doors into a long clinical room. Row upon row of coffin-like structures with glass tops and an electronic control panel at each end filled the room. Most of the units housed the magical creatures; many had markings on their face similar to Garvin's in design. With a loud beeping sound and a small whoosh, the glass tops of twenty-six units slid back. Evidently, Russ had been successful in clearing the device's systems from the control room, allowing the prisoners to escape.

Minutes passed as Marcus and Vara quickly helped the newly awakened to their feet. As was expected, none of them remembered who they were or why they were there. Marcus briefed them as he led the way back through the hallway, meeting up with Russ and Garvin. Vara was behind her people, herding them like lost sheep.

A succession of violent explosions was heard throughout the complex. The building shuddered and pitched, tumbling the people to the floor.

"What the hell was that?" Russ asked of no one in particular.

The ceiling groaned, giving them little warning to scramble out of the way as a large portion of concrete and steel fell, tumbling to the floor in a tremendous crash. Waving away the dust from his face, Marcus stared in disbelief at the pile of rubble now blocking their escape route.

"Is there another way out? A back way?" Garvin asked, getting up from where he landed.

"That was the back way." Russ looked back at the huddled refugees. "Fuck! We'll have to go through the main corridor and fight our way out. Hopefully, the rest of our people are providing enough of a distraction to pull the main security guards away from here." He stepped past them, moving back towards the lab.

"Come on, let's go," Marcus urged the refugees, helping the rest of them to their feet.

Garvin followed Russ, with Marcus leading the refugees, and Vara covering from behind. Russ blasted through
the door at the rear of the lab, leading them through another
office to the open reception area of the facility. What they
found was chaos.

"I don't think it's the security guards we need to worry
about," Vara stated from behind Russ.

Over fifty snarling, half-humans were locked in combat
with each other. Some of the more animal-like beasts were
feeding from the bloody bodies that lay strewn across the
spacious room. Marcus realized that these were more of the
bestial experiments that he and his team had hunted over the
years. The blast from knocking down the doors had alerted
many of them to their presence. Marcus and Russ readied
their guns to shoot their way through the masses, when Garvin
and Vara stepped ahead of them.

Standing side by side they spread their arms wide, static
electricity charging the air. Balling their hands into fists, they
brought their arms straight forward, in front of them. When
their fists contacted, a concussion wave was sent across the
room, knocking down all in its path and slamming into the
walls with such a force that it sent the people behind them
scrambling for purchase.

"Run!" Russ commanded, leading the way to the far wall
where the main exit was clearly marked. Looking out the
skewed doors, he saw that there were no security personnel
in the adjacent room. The wide staircase curved to the upper
level. It's low banister and clear glass wall offered no cover.
They had no choice but to go forward.

Several growls emanated behind them. Russ shifted his
rifle and let loose a barrage of fire covering the escape for the
people. As Marcus and Vara went past him, he focused a few

blasts at cylinders in the corner. The explosions sent flames billowing outward, filing the room. Russ dove through the doors and rolled to his feet. Screams of the few remaining beasts could be heard above the inferno.

Explosions continued in various parts of the building as they climbed the staircase. The building shuddered and rocked beneath their feet, causing many to fall on all fours and scramble up the stairs. Tumbling upon the landing, Marcus turned to help the last of the people off the stairs as it collapsed beneath them. He faced towards the entrance of the building but it wasn't there. A large gaping hole was all that remained of the wall of the building. Beyond the hole, spread out on the manicured lawn, were over a hundred Seds, and all of them had their weapons trained on the group inside.

Shimmers appeared around the entrance hall as Garvin's people phased in from other parts of the building bringing with them the humans. Marcus smiled, with a little satisfaction, as the Seds visibly stepped back from the strange display of power. He knew their fear would not last long. More groups of people materialized behind the Seds.

"Looks like the odds have just evened up," Russ said, charging his rifle and stepping with Garvin into the forefront of the entrance hall.

From behind the Seds, a large purple ball of fire hurtled through the air, landing in the middle of the Seds with a thunderous crash. The Seds scattered, charging the rebels and firing at will. More magical balls of flame, ice and energy in a multitude of colors flew through the air. Many magic shields could be seen blossoming against the energy burst of the Sed's weapons. The rebels were lying on the floor, trying to return fire amidst a hailstorm of magical powers and enemy fire.

Marcus stopped himself from firing as a shield blossomed before him. Unfortunately, the magical shield blocked the energy burst from his gun the same way it did from the Seds' weapons. Marcus looked over at Vara, her face set in grim determination as she wielded the shield to stretch around all of the refugees.

The refugees huddled together, their fear and confusion obvious. Still influenced by the depressant drugs in their system, many of them sat right on the floor where they had fallen during the explosions.

"You are going to have to take them out of here." Marcus shouted over the din of the battle. "They won't be able to help you."

Vara looked at him with reproach. "I can't phase more than three people at a time and I can't do it while still holding a shield around them, we need another way."

Marcus looked for more of the magical people to help him, but they all seemed intent on leading the Seds away from the refugees. Feeling very frustrated, Marcus knew there was no other way, they would have to go through the Seds.

The building shuddered and one of the massive support columns near the rear of the hall fell, scattering people before it. Garvin's people grabbed the rebels and phased out to escape the destruction. The trembling grew, and the ceiling began to collapse.

"We've got move now!" Marcus shouted. Struggling to keep his feet under him, he pulled and pushed several of the refugees forward into the hall following Vera.

Jostled together under the shield, they moved quickly across the open hall straight into a barrage of fire. Several of Garvin's people fell in behind them and phased their people to safety. Within a few minutes, Marcus and Vara stood alone, using part of the remaining wall, just to the side of the breached entrance, as an additional shield blocking them from the Seds view.

Off to the right, Marcus caught sight of Garvin and Russ engaged in a fierce battle with several of the Seds. It seemed all Garvin could do was maintain a shield around him. Russ was hurt, his left arm burned and bloodied. Russ and Garvin took cover behind part of the fallen entrance wall. Blocked from the Seds fire, Garvin moved further back taking a rest and releasing the magical shield. Russ knelt behind one of the smaller boulders and took advantage of having the shield down and returned fire upon the Seds. Marcus noticed a grin spread across Russ's face, his friend was enjoying the payback.

A violently twisting mass of metal structure fell from the ceiling of the hall. It hit with great force, causing the floor to pitch and buck like the devil's own. The flooring supports could not withstand the abuse and broke apart, falling to the levels below and leaving a gaping hole. Tremors increased, large chunks of concrete fell from the walls rolling unto the floor and into the hole. Heavy explosions shook the foundations of the complex. Unable to withstand the abuse, the building's structure was beginning to fail.

Across the hall and the chasm left by the fallen ceiling, Marcus and Vara stared in horror as the wall behind Russ and Garvin slowly gave way. Fissures appeared, creating a crystalline path across the smooth surface of concrete. Rumbling booms accented the widening fractures and pieces splintered off the wall, tumbling down upon the heads of the rebels.

"Russ! Move!" Marcus shouted over the din.

Garvin heard him and phased just in time to miss one of the tumbling boulders, appearing closer to Russ's location. He grabbed Russ just as another portion of the wall came crashing down, obscuring them from Marcus's view.

"No!" Marcus shouted, not sure if they had made it out in time.

"Marcus!" Vara screamed, grabbing his hand and phasing them to the other side of the courtyard beyond the Seds.

"What the hell?" Marcus rounded on her, vertigo forgotten as adrenaline coursed through his veins.

"I had to take us out of there, Marcus, the wall behind us caved in." Vara swung around and pointed at the building.

Marcus looked beyond Vara to the building, just in time to see the rest of the bulk collapse. If anyone hadn't made it out by now, they weren't going to.

"Do you see them?" Marcus asked urgently, pulling his guns up ready to fire if any of the remaining Seds turned in their direction.

"Yes! They're over there on the far side of the yard," Vara whispered fiercely, her brow furrowed in distress.

"Fuck! They're surrounded." Marcus assessed the situation, "Can't your father just phase themselves over here?"

"Not without dropping the shield." Vara stepped out from the shadows, spreading her arms wide, "Get ready to run." She brought her fists forward in a resounding snap, releasing a concussion wave towards the Seds, clearing the area between her and her father.

Recovering his balance from the repercussion of the wave, Marcus waited for the now familiar shimmer to coalesce beside them. He released the breath he did not realize he was holding. They had made it.

"Shit, I'm never going to get used to that," Russ swore, stumbling towards the street.

"Run!" Vara shouted as she threw magical balls of orange energy at the Seds coming into range. Upon impact, they exploded with bright flashes, giving them cover to escape.

Marcus led the way through the streets of Sedia's inner city. Once again cursing the ordered grids of pristine streets and alleyways that offered no. Ironically, they were following the same path that Marcus had chased Vara only a few weeks ago. It seemed like a lifetime had passed since that fateful night. Fumbling in his pocket, he took out his communicator.

"Base! Gateway at warehouse eight, four bio-stamps." Marcus passed the communicator to Russ. Raising his guns, he blasted the newly repaired door to the warehouse.

"There they are!" a voice shouted from down the alleyway. The Seds had found them.

"No time to be nice." Russ opened fire on the Seds as the door finally gave way behind him.

"Come on!" Marcus led the way to the utility door and down the stairs, not bothering with the field dampeners, since the Seds already knew where this gateway was located. The knowledge of any gateway location never did them any good. The gateways could only be activated from base.

The gateway was already formed, its black void beckoning as static electricity flashed around the edges.

"Together now," Marcus placed Vara and Garvin between Russ and him. "Go!"

The four of them entered the bone chilling cold of the gateway's passage. A moment later they tumbled awkwardly from the padded dais.

"Base! Four received. Cut the gateway," Russ urgently shouted into the communicator, rolling away from the tangle of limbs.

The gateway closed with a resounding clap of thunder.

"Looks like we did it." Vara mumbled, more to herself than those present as Garvin helped her to her feet.

Marcus looked at his companions, trying to catch his

breath. Russ leaning against the far wall with his head tilted back and eyes closed. His left arm hung limply at his side, covered with blood and burned where the Sed's blast had glanced off. Vara and Garvin stood quietly side by side, father and daughter of a race alien to Sedia. All were covered with dust, soot and grime. He was sure that he did not look any better. They had just spent the last few hours going through hell and lived to tell about it.

Yes, we did, Marcus thought, out loud he said, "It's not done yet. We need to find out who came back and if there is anyone left on the surface."

Russ groaned when Marcus came up to him. "Fuck, I'm too old for this shit."

Marcus grinned at his old friend, "Hell's fire couldn't have kept you away from this fight. Let's go find Jonas and get you fixed up."

"As long as he's not going to stick me with one of those damn needles," Russ replied, moving away from the wall and falling in step with Marcus.

"Russ, do you think there are any more of those experiments?" Marcus asked in a low voice. It had been nagging at the back of his mind. They had taken out the main science complex but he wasn't sure if there were any other labs that performed genetic experiments. The beasts they had seen in the lower levels of the building were too few in numbers than what they were led to believe from people who used to work for Kelo. There had to be more of them, somewhere.

"I don't think that area we saw was the main facility for those things." Grimacing with pain, Russ paused and holstered his rifle. "When I brought your father down here, he talked of an area that had the capacity to house hundreds of the beasts. They had been in the early stages of planning and the facility had just begun construction. It is possible there are more of those things in Sedia."

"What are we going to do about them?" Marcus wasn't sure why he asked that particular question. They just barely got back with their lives. His heart felt heavy knowing there were more of those beasts to be let loose on Sedia. The rebels wouldn't be here to keep the streets clean or to help those, who stood up to Kelo, escape. It was a sobering thought.

Russ looked over at Marcus, "Not a damn thing."

Marcus keyed into the security panel and pushed open the door to the med-dock. Vara gave him a compassionate look as he held the door open for her and Garvin. She had overheard their conversation.

"Jonas," Marcus called, getting the attention of the medic as he stepped from his office.

"Good to see you're back," Jonas greeted them.

"What's the word? Has everyone else made it back?" Marcus asked the question foremost in his thoughts. He hoped that in spite of the odds all had survived.

"No one was left behind," Jonas answered, frowning. "There were five of our men and one of Garvin's people. They brought the bodies down here, and one of my medics is tending to their remains."

"Damn." Russ swore, after Jonas named those that had made it back.

"And the rest?" Marcus prompted.

"Most came through with minor bumps and bruises, three with broken bones but will be mobile in a few hours. My team has removed the last of the devices from the refugees and they should start waking up in two hours. Everyone else has been sent to the surface." Jonas looked at Russ. "Follow me and let's take a look at your arm."

"It's not your fault, you know." Vara walked beside Marcus, a little behind Russ and Gavin as they followed Jonas to the last active med-dock in the facility.

"What do you mean?" Marcus asked. He had known it would be risky when they took so many people on the surface. Still, he should have thought of a better attack plan. Maybe then his friends would still be alive.

"You are not responsible for those that have fallen. They went into the battle willingly." Vara laid a comforting hand on his arm. "Grieve, but do not blame yourself."

"How did you know?" Marcus asked, startled that she had read his thoughts.

"I have gotten to know you these last few weeks. When we leave this place, I would like to travel with you and your people as they find their new home." Vara looked up at him. "If it is all right with you."

Marcus grinned down at her. "Yes, I would like that."

* * *

"Is this the last of the supplies?" Marcus asked, shifting the medical cases they would be taking with them into the alcove of the back tunnel.

"Yes." Jonas looked down at his clipboard checking the cases off his list. "All that is left is to evacuate the people from the med-dock. It feels strange to leave a place I called home all my life. Thankfully there had been enough salvaged parts to make two transits to carry my equipment."

"And carry the supplies to get us across the desert," Marcus reminded him. He straightened, holding up a hand to quiet Jonas. He thought he heard something coming from the upper base. He felt a slight tremor as sand sifted from the roof of the lower catacombs.

"What the hell?" Marcus swore. He turned and sprinted

up the walkways to the base, leaving Jonas far behind.

He saw a dozen Seds swarming on the upper platform. They had found a way into the rebel's base. He had left Vara and Garvin in the med-dock with the refugees. Anger coursed through his veins. After everything that had happened, they were not going to take away his home. Through his fury he did not reason that he was leaving it anyway.

Quickly and silently Marcus made his way down the corridors, stalking one Sed after another, dispatching each one before there was a chance to alert the others. Efficent. Deadly. He cautiously approached the corner to the med-dock. Lights flickered along the wall from the discharges of the Seds' weapons. The blasts reverberated through the corridors, masking any sounds Marcus made.

He checked his guns for a full power clip and readied himself. Taking a deep breath he turned the corner and fired.

Vara and Garvin were pressed back against the med-dock doors. Their shields were pounded relentlessly by the Seds' fire. Marcus cut through the unsuspecting Seds, his wrath unleashed. Each shot was precise and set to kill, dropping the Seds before they had time to react to his presence.

Marcus stood looking over the bodies. Adrenaline rushed through his veins and his chest heaved, trying to catch his breath. He jumped when he felt something touch him. Spinning around, he raised his guns ready to fire. He saw a shield blossom before him and Vara smiling wryly.

"Sorry," Marcus apologized, stepping back and lowering his weapons. "I don't think that's all of them. Let's get these people out of here. You two will guard and shield them until they are safely in the tunnel. I'll make sure our retreat is cleared."

He entered the key code to the med-dock and opened

the door to find the refugees had already assembled to leave. Some of the people were holding makeshift gurneys to carry the injured. Vara led the way with the refugees in the middle and Garvin at the rear. Their shields stretched over them, melding in the middle creating a solid dome. Marcus followed outside the shield, constantly searching for any Seds.

Upon reaching the lower caverns, Marcus observed more Seds coming through the base's platform and starting down the causeway to the lower caverns.

"Go!" Marcus shouted, opening fire on the Seds.

Vara led the way to the residences and ducked into the narrow walkways, disappearing from view. Almost pushing against Garvin's shield, Marcus emptied his clip into the Seds, covering their retreat. Once around the corner, he reloaded his guns. Looking back, he saw Jonas and Vara helping people into the tunnel.

Garvin released his shield and stood next to Marcus, his face grave. "They cannot be allowed to follow us," he stated calmly.

"How are we going to stop them?" Marcus asked, staring at the corner where the Seds would emerge.

"I will collapse the cavern. Vara will make sure you and your people are safe in the tunnels," Garvin replied.

"I'm staying." Marcus left no room for argument. Garvin would need his protection as he wielded the magic. He turned and locked eyes with Vara. He hoped she understood what he was asking of her. If he didn't make it, she would lead Russ and his people to their new home. With a slight nod of her head, she disappeared into the tunnel closing the door behind her.

"Let's go." Marcus led Garvin towards the common area of the cavern. He took a circuitous route through the warren of personal residences, eerily empty and abandoned by their occupants. If Garvin succeeded, it would be the last time he would ever see them.

"Here," he whispered, stopping at an entrance to the common area located at the far side of the cavern and shrouded in shadows. The cavern's vaulted rock roof made even the smallest sound echo. Across the basin, he could see the Seds milling around the base and the corridor to the tunnel. He hoped this would work. Remembering the backlashes from the concussion waves, he stood back letting Garvin have a clear area around him. Charging his guns, he was ready.

Garvin raised his hands to his sides, head thrown back, and his feet spread. His long silver hair lifted as the air charged with static. His hands glowed a dark purple light, a light that absorbed all other light. He brought his hands in front of him and created a sphere of this light. Shades of purple danced within the globe, streaks of silver and black laced through it. Faster and faster the colors swirled as it grew, doubling in size. With a rush of sound that sounded like wind howling through the tunnels, Garvin launched the sphere straight at the caverns roof.

The Seds opened fire at the globe and did not notice them still standing in the shadows of the far corner of the cavern. The sphere absorbed the energy of the shots, growing larger. It hit the ceiling with a thunderous boom. Walls tumbled and rocks fell, the Seds scrambled for footing.

Losing his balance, Marcus went down to one knee. He glanced up at the ceiling, expecting it to be falling. It wasn't. The purple had spread across the entire dome, the colors swirling and occasionally flashing red lightning-like streaks through it. He looked around at the Seds, they too were staring up at the ceiling.

"Get ready to run," Gavin told him in a low voice. Once again his arms were spread wide. This time he brought them forward and up, letting go a powerful concussion wave. Seconds later, the deafening rumble of the rock breaking up filled the cavern echoing off the rock wall.

Garvin helped Marcus to his feet, "Go!"

Marcus didn't argue, racing along the walkways of the residences back towards the tunnel. The residence structures were swaying drunkenly, collapsing in heaps of rubble. The stone pitched and heaved around them as the heavy chunks of ceiling fell to the floor of the catacombs. Marcus lunged for the door to the tunnel and opened it for Garvin to go through first. Slamming it behind him, Marcus set the wheel-lock, just as something crashed on the other side.

Cracks appeared in the ceiling as Marcus dashed after Garvin who was wielded a shield to protect them from the occasional falling rocks. It was several minutes before the trembling stopped. Relieved, Marcus saw Vara and the refugees ahead of him.

Twelve grueling hours later, they arrived at the rendezvous point. The exhausted people sat against the tunnel walls waiting for their turn to phase to the surface. The last to leave, Marcus phased with Vara to the surface desert and experienced his first view of Sedia from outside its walls.

Exhilaration filled him as he looked over the seemingly never-ending expanse of desert in the failing evening light. Nothing marred the horizon, giving him the sense of being very small in a large world. A soft breeze caressed his face as he grinned and breathed deep the fresh air. Marcus was amazed at the clear quality of the air compared to the recycled air of the dome.

"Welcome to the outside," Vara said softly, looking up at Marcus.

Marcus looked back at Sedia. The destruction of the catacombs had caused many of the city's towering buildings to collapse. Fires had erupted, spewing immense clouds of smoke and soot into the air only to be captured by the dome, blackening parts of it. The parts that were clear of the soot glowed orange from the light cast from the fires. It created a disturbing image against the night sky as if hell itself had woken and shown its hand in Sedia.

He knew that someday he would return to finish what had been started this day. He looked at the caravan that stretched out over the sands away from Sedia. This was his future, now he needed to take care of the people. The free people of Sedia.

"Ofelia's Avocado"
("Yes, that's not your…)
ChaosInOrder

I peer at the rough covering
but it's impossible to know
if the flesh underneath is ready
the inverted pear looks ripe
to the naked eye
tempting, tantalizing
bringing sweet juices to my mouth
cold box protects it
but the door
is open

Is it mine?
knowledge comes from nerve
nerve asks questions
nerve looks
probing with the eye first
the answer not arriving
it *looks* like mine

it *looks* ripened
ready
to be split open

nerve must be sated
answer must be known

to touch
to caress and squeeze gently
the only path nerve knows
to answer the question
nerve learned this from desire
and desire never lies to nerve

he reaches towards the covering
desire driving nerve
in an instant
knowledge is attained…

SMACK!

"That is so **NOT** your…

…Avocado."

The Phoenix
Tracy Crowe

She flies wearily across the sea
Searching for a place to land
Her flesh is burning hot and cold
She feels the flames rising
In her heart
Soon she will die
In a thunderous flash
And all the old
Will be forgotten
And the past will grow cold
She longs for the darkness
To wrap around her
Like a warm blanket
To swallow the sorrow and toil

She sees in the distance
The mountain where she was born
She remembers well
The trials of coming from darkness
Into light

Learning to fly
And falling falling falling
Down time after time
It seems an eternity ago
That she first alighted
From her home
To wander the world
Of magic, mystery and shame

Her weary feet land
On the cold mountain stone
The winter has come
And it has stayed too long
The tears begin to flow
And become a river
Soaked up by the parched ground
The time has finally come
She burns she burns she burns
Inside and out
A burst of flame and light
And she is gone.

The darkness encompasses her
And she is no more.
The wind howls her name
In a grieving song
And then all is silent.
The darkness cradles her for eternity
The sweetness of nothing
Heals all her aches
The balm of timelessness
A salve to her wounds

All the sins are forgotten
And thrown into the ocean of forever.
The dark is long and silent
And she breathes a sigh of relief.

The morning breaks bright and clear
In hues of purple, red and blue
The breeze whispers of a new day
A single blade of grass begins to
Poke through the dry earth
Where yesterday the tears fell
In the silence there is a faint rushing sound
Like the pounding of a tiny heartbeat
Soft at first

Then
A gasp of breath
Lungs sucking in air and life
And from the ashes she arises

For she is reborn.

Never Dance With Janis
In The Front Seat
ChaosInOrder

Ok, so I think this country is pretty screwy these days. That was true even before I became homeless two months ago. I think it's the fault of the people for allowing it to happen over the last 40 years. I have no problem spoutin' my mouth off just about anytime I see an example of the screwyness. And I also really enjoy pointing out the good, the cool, the serendipitous that is being human, and occasionally American. Those two things are not exclusory of each other. Serendipitous situations can happen anywhere, no matter how bad the living conditions may be or how stupid and mean the people are. But it's not very often that I say, "Hey, at least for a brief shining moment today, I was wrong. This country isn't so bad, and Americans can be nice."

Hey, for a brief shining moment this morning, I was damn glad I'm a citizen of these United States, and some folks I would not have expected it from were nice to me.

One of the first things my friend and mentor in the urban vagabond world, Bert, taught me, was that you never sleep sitting up in the driver's seat. If you do, you become a sitting duck for law enforcement, and maybe more importantly than a sitting duck, a pain in the ass. Think about it…you're a cop on patrol in the urban ghetto. You see a body slumped forward, or laid head back, in the driver's seat of a parked car. First thought? C'mon…you guys watch *The Sopranos*. Dead, or dead drunk. Cops don't like dead bodies or dead drunks; the former smells bad and creates mountains of paperwork…the latter…heh…well, yeah, same thing, plus it wakes up and gives you shit. Any self respecting urban vagabond realizes that the cops are his friend till he pisses them off, and the best way to not piss a cop off is to stay the hell out of his or her field of vision, to try to blend into the masses of the society you are trying like hell to get out of. So, you don't sleep sitting up in the driver's seat.

I wrote till about 3:30 this morning. I was planning to just keep it going, but I'm not really driving the creative vehicle lately, my characters are. Nurse Jenny had put in her thousand words, and The Dancer was deep in thought, so I shut the laptop down, packed it into the Amazon.com backpack, and walked out of the 24 hour bowling alley I call home these days, and headed out to the K car motel. The universe, in the form of a leggy 30-something with a nice rack who would have been more than welcome on my head pin, had left me half a pack of American Spirits in the banana box, and when I got to the car I decided to enjoy a cigarette. I never smoke in the bedroom, so I crawled into the front room (seat) and prepared to light up. Before I could do that, however, The Dancer started jibber-jabbering. He keeps bugging me to let him go to the Newport Festival in '65 so he can be the first person to dance while Dylan plays electric. I keep telling him the rooftop thing with The Beatles was grandiose enough for the time being, but he said he had talked to Janis and she was into it...the little bastard knows I can't resist Joplin in a see through halter top, so away we went. Janis was in fine form, still on her first fifth of Jack for the day, and she was doing the electric boogaloo all over The Dancer's leg, her tits bouncing up and down, supercharged little mountains of electric lust as the crowd began to boo Dylan and his electric guitar, and rock and roll history began to unfold on the stage twenty feet in front of them. The Dancer's hands came down from behind his head and reached for the soft pink of Joplin's taut n—

BAM BAM BAM. My eyes flung themselves open and then squinted at the bright light hiding a barely seen apparition in blue on the other side of the K car Motel's passenger side window.

"HEY..." BAM BAM, "Hey, wake up!"

"I'm awake, officer."

The passenger door opened and the face of the man ducked in. What are you doing in there, sir? Are you hurt?"

"No...no, just fell asleep, I guess."

"Do you have some identification, sir?"

"Um, yeah, sure. Can I get out and give it to you?" For some reason my first desire whenever I've been pulled over is to get out of the car.

"No, stay right there, just give me your I.D., please."

Wide awake and hyperaware, I realized I wasn't hearing anything threatening from the voice of the man, but at the same time I realized there was not just one, or two police vehicles on the scene, but three. "Ok, sure. No prob." I pulled my genuine Italian leather wallet, a gift from a friend who had been in Italy a few years ago, out of my back pocket, opened it up on top of the suitcase that occupied the passenger side of the K car, and pulled my driver's license out. As he took my license, the man said, "So, you living in the vehicle, sir?"

"Yeah."

"Ok…hang on right here, I'll be right back."

I know there's nothing untoward on my record, so as I waited for the man to return, I was more chagrined than anything else. Bert's car/home is a scant thirty yards to the left, and my predominant thought was, "Shit. Bert's gonna kill me." By letting down my guard, by letting The Dancer be more enamored with Bob Dylan changing the history of popular music, and with Janis Joplin's tits, than our survival, I had inadvertently put Bert's existence in jeopardy as well. I hear the man close the door of his cruiser and hear him call out, "Clean as a whistle, no surprise." Cruisers 2 and 3 immediately leave the scene and the man came back to the K car Motel. "Here you go, Mr. D**, the reason we stopped is that we drove by awhile and your car was running, then we came back by and it wasn't, but you were kinda slumped over in the seat…just wanted to make sure you were ok…you are ok, right?"

"Yes, sire, and I really am trying to get this thing out of here."

"No worries, sir," the man *smiled*, "go back to sleep. Just try to make it to the back seat, ok?"

"Yeah, absolutely." His flashlight was off and we were having real eye contact in the soft light of the car's interior. "Thank you."

"Not a problem. Have a good day."
"Thanks, you too."

Only in America, and God—whichever one you believe in—bless her for it.

Dragon Hunted
Angie Mansfield

A high, lilting voice filtered through the trees. Lairn paused, frowning in the dim starlight. Hoping the racket would not alert his quarry, he reached for the unfamiliar hilt of his new sword and broke into a clearing.

In the center of the small glen sat a slender blonde woman. The half-moon cast little light, but enough fell on her face to allow Lairn to recognize her. She winked, took a deep swig from the bottle in her hand, belched in a most unladylike manner, then belted out the next verse of a randy drinking song.

Lairn huffed in disgust. "One would think, Sayla, that the daughter of a queen, and an elf besides, would comport herself with more dignity."

Green eyes glittered in the scant starlight as she cut off the song in mid-verse. "I'll thank you to piss off, dragon killer," she slurred, then took another drink.

A great sigh escaped his lips as he stepped over her and headed for the trees on the opposite side of the clearing. "Fine. Call me whatever you like. I'm only doing my job."

"Sure you are," she muttered, making two attempts before

hauling herself to unsteady feet. "But you *love* your job, don't you? Hmm? Murderer." The accusation dissolved into curses as she gestured too broadly with the hand holding the bottle, sloshing some of the white liquid to the ground.

"It would be wise to quiet down," Lairn suggested, studying the forest again. He had been tracking the dragon for two days, and had gained considerable ground. The creature was not far ahead of him. He hoped it would not decide to investigate the noise.

"Hey! Kill-dragon! I'm not done speaking to you!"

"Quiet, you little fool! Do you want to end up a pile of cooked meat?"

Laughter bubbled from her throat, and she stumbled off into the woods before he could reach out to stop her. Lairn frowned and drew his sword. Damned elves and their unicorn milk! Worse than a troll with a whole keg of fire brandy. Shaking his head, he pushed through the undergrowth and followed her, paying close attention to the surrounding forest.

He had only followed a few steps of Sayla's staggering, grumbling progress when he heard thrashing in the trees to his left. Whatever approached was making too much noise to be the elf princess. Loud pops and cracks marked its splintering rush through the woods. A soft breeze stirred, carrying the acrid scent of ash and sulfur to Lairn's nose.

The dragon.

It was headed in Sayla's direction. Lairn dropped into a crouch, hand aching from his tense grip on the sword. The wizard who'd sold him the blade told him it was enchanted to kill a dragon with the first blow. Lairn didn't know why he'd bought the thing; he hated magic. He hoped the blasted thing would work.

Sayla's voice carried a curse over the sounds of her unseen stalker. "Are you listening to me?" she shouted.

A roar greeted her words, followed by a blinding flash of light and a wave of heat that threatened to knock Lairn flat. Cursing, he charged toward Sayla's last angry shout.

"Whad'ja do that for?"

Relief rushed through him when he heard the petulant voice whining at the dragon. He did not relish the thought of explaining to the elf queen how he'd allowed her eldest daughter to be roasted alive. The last time he'd faced that cold woman had been enough.

Sayla's next words made him grin, in spite of himself.

"I was trying to defend you, you big bag of cinders!"

Hacking through the undergrowth, Lairn found Sayla swaying like a leaf in a hurricane. She glared up at the dragon, shook her fist at it, and took another pull from the bottle. The trees around her were blackened and still smoking.

Taking a deep breath, Lairn released his battle cry, put his most intimidating look on his face, and charged. He leaped across the last few feet and struck at the beast, putting all his strength behind the blow.

With a sound like breaking glass, the sword shattered and fell in glittering shards to the ground. Lairn was left holding a few inches of jagged metal protruding from a jewel-encrusted hilt. He stared stupidly at it for a moment, then up at the dragon as it turned with deliberate slowness to glare at him.

Laughter distracted them both. Sayla held her sides with both arms, cackling until she fell on her backside.

"Oooh," she gasped, swiping at the tears of laughter running down her cheeks. "You sure slew that one, big boy! Momma will be so proud!"

Rolling his eyes and hoping the dragon couldn't run as fast as it could fly, Lairn grabbed the drunk elven princess, tossed her over his shoulder, swallowed the bit of pride he had left, and ran.

* * *

Hard ground under her back, something soft under her head.

Oh, her head!

Moaning, Sayla raised a heavy arm to place her hand on her forehead. Even with her eyes closed, the light shining on her face was too bright. Her tongue felt swollen and dry.

Steeling herself, she opened one eye and immediately regretted it. Sunlight pierced her pupil, aggravating the throbbing ache in her head. She tried to roll onto her side and was overcome with a wave of nausea.

"Not feeling well this morning, eh?"

Lairn's deep voice vibrated through her skull, making her dizzy. "Not so loud," she pleaded, pressing both hands to her temples.

He chuckled. "Never thought I'd see you sick with drink, princess."

"Speak with more respect," she managed to croak, pondering the difficult task of sitting up. "You no longer have the right to be so familiar."

"Ever the romantic," he said, humor gone from his voice. Sayla felt strong hands on her shoulders, and did not resist as he helped her sit up. She waited for the nausea and dizziness to subside, then tried opening her eyes again.

They were in a cave. Stone walls narrowed toward a gash in the rock that allowed the sunlight to penetrate their hiding spot.

"Where are we?"

"The best place I could find while hauling an unconscious drunken elf over my shoulder and running from an
enraged dragon." Lairn moved to sit on the other side of the
cramped space, dark eyes studying her.

"Ugh, the dragon," Sayla said, as the fuzzy memory of
shouting at the creature drifted through her mind. "Did I really shake my fist at it?"

Lairn's tanned face split into a wide grin. "And called
him a 'big bag of cinders', I believe."

Sayla glared at him. "I'm glad you find this so amusing."

"It's always amusing to see you fall on your backside,
my dear."

"A bit like watching you trying to charm the pretty young
things at Fair time," she snapped. She regretted the words
even before Lairn's face darkened and he turned away. Why
did she feel this need to hurt him?

"We're stuck here for awhile," he said through clenched
teeth. "Perhaps it would be best if we keep to ourselves."

"Surely it's gone away by now."

"Ha. You obviously don't know a thing about the creatures you claim to love so much."

"So why don't you teach me?"

"Oh, the great elf princess wants the lowly human hunter
to teach her something, does she?" He turned to glare at her.
"You weren't so interested in anything I had to say while we
were married, my dear."

"You never had anything interesting to say," she snapped,
forgetting the shame she'd felt a few moments before. "Killing is everything to you."

"That's not true, and you know it." He leaned forward,
nearly touching noses with her, glaring into her eyes. "I became

a hunter to support you when your mother tossed you out for marrying a dirty *human*. I took the jobs no one else wanted, because those jobs were the only ones that paid enough to maintain your level of comfort. I killed innocent creatures whose only sin was possessing magic...and I did all of it for you, princess. Love your dragons all you want. But remember that dozens of them have died to buy you pretty clothes and precious gems for those dainty fingers."

Tears burned her eyes, but a wave of nausea prevented her reply. Her stomach heaved violently, and she scuttled to the back of the cave to be sick.

After a moment, Lairn sighed. The rustle of clothing told her he'd moved to her side, and gentle hands gathered her hair behind her head. She was glad he had the decency not to comment.

* * *

She went back to sleep a few minutes after emptying her stomach. Lairn leaned his back against the rough stone wall and watched her, remembering how she had been before things had become...unpleasant.

The five years since their wedding had aged them both. Sayla's mother had disowned her, tossing the princess into a despair that had etched worry lines around her eyes and mouth. Lairn's forced hunting of creatures he once admired - and the accident that had destroyed their marriage - had weathered him.

He hadn't been fair to her, of course. She'd never asked for the life he'd tried to give her. She had turned her back on the world she knew, the destiny she had been born to, all for him. He had been the one who'd insisted on the fancy clothes and expensive trinkets.

He didn't deserve her, never had, and his failed attempt

to measure up through monetary gain was the true source of the bitter contempt with which he now regarded himself. It wasn't Sayla's fault; he was the one who'd failed her. He was glad her mother had relented after the marriage fell apart; was relieved that she had allowed Sayla back into the life she'd tried to deny.

But he resented his former wife, too, just a bit. She had a life to go back to. He had nothing but the legend he'd made of himself as a dragonslayer. *Now I'm the one being hunted,* he thought in dark amusement, glancing at the cave entrance.

As if reading his thoughts, his scaled captor rumbled a challenge. Lairn frowned at the broken sword he'd inexplicably carried with him on his mad flight from the dragon. *Fat lot of good it does me now*, he thought, kicking at the offending blade.

"Shouldn't you be focusing your energy on getting us out of here?" Sayla pulled herself upright as she spoke, stretching.

Frustration boiled to the surface, but he held it in check. "Got any ideas?" he said, managing to keep a civil tone.

"You're the great dragon hunter." She winced. Green eyes, the depthless hue that had first drawn him to her, met his. "I'm sorry. I don't know what's wrong with me."

Damn. Two years of separation and resentment, and he still couldn't resist those eyes. He took a deep breath and smiled. "It's all right."

She turned her attention to the cave entrance. "How long will he sit out there?"

"Longer than we can sit in here." He nudged his pack toward her. "I've got a bit of food, if you're hungry. Nothing fancy, but it should soothe your stomach."

Slender fingers pulled the pack to her, and she nodded

gratefully. "So how do we get out?"

"Well, that's the question of the day, isn't it?" Frustration made his voice sharper than he'd intended.

"I was only asking a question!"

"And if I knew the answer to it, don't you think we'd be out of here by now?"

For a moment, they glared at each other across the small cave. Sayla gave in first.

"All right, I'm sorry. I guess I just thought you might have been in a situation like this before and have some trick to get us past him. Perhaps there's a back way out of the cave?"

He rubbed his temple with one hand. "I checked that while you were asleep. The cave leads through the mountain and meets a hundred other tunnels and caverns on the way. There's a stream that runs through the main path, and it might lead us out, but there's no way to be sure the whole tunnel doesn't disappear under water." Scowling at the sword, he said, "That was my spectacular trick. It's supposed to be indestructible, the ultimate dragon hunting weapon. Guess I'll learn not to trust a wizard."

Sayla's eyes narrowed, and she picked up the broken weapon. When her fingers brushed over the jeweled hilt, she dropped it, shaking her hand as though she'd been burned.

"What's wrong?" Lairn leaned forward.

Her face paled as she met his gaze. "That thing is filled with magic," she said, "but not the kind that's harmful to dragons."

"So some old wizard sold me a defective magical sword," he said, not understanding her reaction. "I would think you'd get plenty of amusement out of that fact."

Shaking her head, she nudged the blade toward the back

of the cave with one foot. "You don't understand. It's not just defective. It was designed to lead you -"

"To a dragon, I know," he interrupted.

"No. To an elf." Drawing her knees up under her chin, she glanced at the cave entrance and shuddered. "It's also acting as a beacon, leading its owner to us. I've seen this sword before. It was used in an assassination attempt several months ago. Kiel, Father's old court wizard, showed it to me. I didn't tell you before, because we were fighting, but..." Haunted eyes met his.

"Someone is trying to kill me."

* * *

Fear writhed in her stomach, souring the bit of food Lairn had given her. She could still feel the cold, greasy magic from the sword, and she wiped her hand on her leg for the hundredth time. How many attempts on her life did this make? Three? Four? She cursed herself for being so stupid. She should have stayed with the guards, like she'd been told. But then Kiel had produced the unicorn milk, and they drank to her father's memory.

Of course, he'd only been trying to get her drunk so she would wander away from the protection of the guards. All the better if the dragon finished her; then it would be an accident. Otherwise, he still had the sword, which Lairn would carry to find the dragon...and Sayla.

Lairn crouched at the cave entrance, studying the dragon and the surrounding woods to find a way out or spot signs of their pursuer. Sayla was glad he was here with her. Whatever their past, he was good at his work, and she felt safer with him than with an entire troop of her mother's guards.

"We've got to try the tunnels," he said, returning.

"But you said -"

"I know what I said." His voice was gentle, soothing her nerves. "That was before I knew someone - and we can't be sure it's Kiel - intends to use me to find and kill you. Anyone hunting us has only to find his way past that dragon to get in here and finish the job. The only weapon I have left is a dagger. We're trapped, a perfect target." He put one hand on her shoulder and gave it a light squeeze. "It won't be easy, and I'm not sure we can find the way, Sayla. But we can't just sit here and wait for death."

She nodded, mesmerized by his eyes. Calm, steady Lairn. Even after all the bad blood, she found herself trusting him without question. He would get her out of here or die trying.

He turned away to retrieve his pack, and the moment was broken. Sayla stood up and stared at the sunlight pouring through the cave entrance. She drank in the sight, wondering how much time would pass before she would feel its warm rays on her face again.

"Time to go," Lairn said, lighting a torch. "We'll have to be quick; I only have three of these."

She nodded and followed him, squeezing through a crack in the cave's rear wall.

They left the sword, unwilling to touch it after Sayla had discovered its purpose.

* * *

Lairn paused, raising his hand to motion Sayla to silence. He strained his ears, trying to decipher the noise he'd just heard.

There. A small scrape, a rustle that sounded like clothing on rough rock. A quick glance at Sayla's wide eyes told him she'd heard it too. The twisting passages amplified sounds, bouncing them off the rock walls so that it was impossible to tell the direction from which the noise had come.

Sayla slipped her hand into his, the last traces of hostility gone from both of them. Hoping he could get her out of this alive, he moved on. A plan began to form in his mind, and he started searching for just the right place to carry it out.

He found it a few minutes later, at the convergence of two narrower tunnels. On the right hand side, just before the tunnels branched, was a hollowed-out space in the wall. A few large rocks sat in front of the opening, making it visible from the branches, but mostly hidden from the direction they'd come. Pulling Sayla close, he whispered in her ear.

"I need you to get inside, and move as far back as you can."

She nodded, and slipped into the hole. Holding his torch up as if he were traveling normally through the tunnel, he could not see her in the space. Satisfied, he motioned her out, and whispered to her again.

"I need you to do exactly as I tell you, with no questions," he said. "I'm going to hide here and wait for our friend. I need you to keep going, let him hear you moving, so he will continue to follow. When he comes past me, I'll stop him."

Wide eyes sought his. Motioning for his ear, she whispered, "What if you're unable to stop him?"

"Then keep following the water. It will lead you out. Don't move slowly in the hopes that I'll catch up. If I'm successful, I'll find you outside. If not, go home and don't wait for me."

Tears formed in her eyes, and he wanted to erase the intervening years, sweep her back to the day they were married, and start over. Before he could change his mind, he kissed her softly on the mouth, pressed the torch into her hand, and nudged her toward the right-hand tunnel. She nodded, turned, and left, not looking back.

Darkness followed in her wake.

* * *

Sayla wiped her eyes, willing herself to remain strong...and to forget about that kiss until they both were safe.

She distracted herself by thinking about the identity of their pursuer. Her magic had never been strong like her mother's; perhaps she was mistaken about the weapon's purpose and origins. Except...

Except she knew she wasn't mistaken. Kiel had shown it to her after the last failed murder plot. He had been cold and resentful since she'd returned, and she knew he blamed her for her father's death. And it had been partly her fault, she admitted, as much as it had been Lairn's or her father's himself. They'd have had no reason to quarrel, and her father would not have been on that mountain, had it not been for her and her childish tantrums. Her face burned in shame at the way she'd been, prideful and selfish. No wonder Lairn had let her go so easily.

She slipped through a narrow spot in the tunnel, and halted. A few steps ahead of her, the ceiling had given way to the pressure of the tons of rock above it. The creek bubbled cheerfully into and between the rocks, unfazed by the blockage. Sayla, however, had nowhere to go.

Now what?

* * *

Crouching in his hole, Lairn forced himself to focus on the tunnel. He would not allow Sayla's would-be killer to pass this point. The thought of her face, frozen in death, chilled him. Bad enough he'd let her father fall that day.

Movement caught his attention. Gripping the dagger, he tensed, wishing he had a more substantial weapon.

Light touched the wall, and a hand holding a torch came into Lairn's view. The torch stopped just in front of Lairn's hole, then made its way toward the tunnel Sayla had taken. He held his breath, crept from cover, and brandished the dagger. He was about to call out when the other man broke the silence.

"That isn't very nice." Lairn jumped as the man turned to face him.

"Kiel."

"So good to see you again," the wizard said. He dropped the torch, plunging them into darkness.

Lairn ducked and stepped to the side, unable to make out the slightest detail in the perfect black of the cave.

Something hit him, hard, in the back of the head, and bright spots of light exploded in front of his eyes. He slumped forward, on hands and knees, trying to shake off the blow and regain his senses.

The wizard chuckled. "Magic gives you good night vision," he said, and kicked Lairn in the ribs.

Gasping for breath, Lairn lay on the cold stone floor, listening for indications of the wizard's position.

"Thanks for helping me find your pretty former bride," Kiel said. His voice echoed, and Lairn could not determine his location.

Something heavy hit him in the head. Pain sent him into a darkness blacker than the cave's gloom.

* * *

Sayla heard voices, far away and muffled, like a whisper under water. She ignored them, pushing herself another few inches.

She had discovered that the collapsed ceiling did not fill the entire tunnel; a small space remained near the left wall. It was narrow, but she managed to squeeze into it. She had to extinguish the torch, and she wasn't sure how she was going to navigate the rest of the way out. Refusing to think about it, she pulled herself another inch, two, and her head was out the other side. Fresh air touched her face.

Hoping that the fresh air indicated the exit and not just a small fissure in the rock, she lowered herself to the tunnel floor. She had scraped one shoulder in her climb, and her shirt was torn, but she had made it.

Darkness still pressed on her, and she was forced to creep along the passage, hands out to avoid obstacles. She used her toes to test the ground, and followed the draft on her face. Her fingers brushed against rock as she came to a bend in the tunnel, and she groped around for a moment before realizing that she could see dim outlines of the rocks. To the left, the tunnel brightened, and the draft was now a breeze. Pace quickened in anticipation, she hurried around one last bend and found a large cave mouth, with sunlight pouring through.

Smiling, she stepped out onto a stone ledge, breathing deep lungfuls of the fresh air.

Hoping Lairn was right behind her, she began to work her way down the cliff to a deer trail below.

* * *

Pain woke him. He tried to lift his head, but the movement sent pain knifing through his chest; he had to grit his teeth to keep from crying out. He could not open his right eye; when he touched it, his fingers came away sticky. Tearing a piece of his shirt, he made a makeshift bandage around his head, and hoped the blood would dry before he got outside. Dragons were attracted to the scent, and the last thing he and Sayla needed...

Sayla.

The thought of her shocked him fully awake. Bracing himself, he pushed up on his hands and knees, and had to fight off a wave of nausea. He staggered to his feet and tried to get his bearings, but the unrelenting black of the cave disoriented him.

Think. Which way did I turn when I left the hole?

Feeling his way blindly, he bumped into the rocks in front of the space that had hidden him. He turned left, keeping one hand on the wall to guide himself, and began following Sayla and the wizard.

* * *

She crouched behind the cover of a fallen tree and watched the cave, wishing Lairn would hurry. Her nerves were wound tight, making her jumpy.

Movement at the cave mouth stirred her hopes for a moment, then dashed them when Kiel stepped out instead of Lairn.

Why don't I ever do what they tell me? she berated herself, fear quickening her breath. She crept backwards, hoping to slip away before the wizard caught sight of her.

He began to make his way down the cliff face before her view was obscured by trees. Finding the deer path, she ran.

Just past a sharp turn in the path, he stepped out of the trees in front of her. Hands like steel bands wrapped around her wrists, holding her still.

"What are you doing out here all by yourself, Your Highness?"

She glared up at him. "Let me go."

"Go? Where? Back to your precious dragon hunter? Ha. If he makes it out of the caves alive, he'll be the one hunted. Dragon hunter, dragon hunted." He laughed at his joke. "Dragons can smell blood from miles away, did you know that?"

Cold fear stole into her heart. Blood? She knew something must have happened to Lairn if Kiel made it out of the caves, but the word "blood" sent chills through her anyway.

"He's not coming for you," the wizard said.

Tears burned her eyes. "Why are you doing this? I know you were close to Father, but I never meant to hurt him."

He laughed. "You think this is about that old fool?" Releasing one of her hands, he reached into the bag at his hip and withdrew a rope. "Hold still, or I'll cut you," he said, showing her the dagger in his belt.

Why start listening now? she thought. She snatched the dagger with her free hand, and turned it toward his belly.

He shoved her backward and pointed at the dagger. It jerked free of her grip and buried itself in a nearby tree.

"You always were stubborn," he said, and the sly amusement was gone. He snatched her wrists again, tying the rope with quick, angry movements. "Scores of elven men for you to choose from, and you had to be *difficult*. Had to marry a *human*."

"What?" The change in the conversation's direction confused her.

"Quiet!" He grabbed a handful of her hair and pulled her face close, nose to nose. "My son was among the men you scorned. You didn't even have the decency to tell him yourself; you had your *maid* do it for you!"

Sayla tried to shake her head, but his grip tightened on her hair. She held back a cry of pain, afraid it would encourage him to further violence. "I'm sorry," she said.

He slapped her, hard, and now she did cry out. Tears of pain escaped the corners of her eyes.

Kiel shoved, putting one toe behind her foot to trip her. She landed hard on her backside. Slivers of pain stabbed through her back.

He knelt beside her and put one hand around her throat, squeezing enough to make her wheeze for breath.

"No one will find you out here. My face will be the last one you see." His hand tightened, cutting off her air. Dark patches floated in front of her eyes as she clawed at his wrist with her tied hands.

* * *

Lairn charged through the trees, terrified that he would find her too late. The pain in his ribs stabbed him with every step, but he forced himself to ignore it.

So consumed was he in his running that he almost missed the sound above him. By the time he identified it as wings beating air, the dragon was directly overhead.

Without slowing, he reached up and pulled the cloth off his head, wincing when he saw it saturated with blood. The dragon roared, driven mad by the scent.

Lairn leapt over a small bush and skidded to a halt. He was in the middle of the deer trail. Kiel had his back to him, kneeling over Sayla with his hand around her throat.

The wizard heard Lairn behind him and rose, turning to meet the new threat. Thinking quickly, Lairn jumped forward, closing the distance between them. He stuffed the cloth into the front pocket of the wizard's tunic and shoved him backwards. The dragon roared another warning. Lairn heard the intake of breath as the creature prepared to incinerate the area.

Sayla doubled over, gagging, when Kiel let go of her throat. Lairn grabbed her arm, pulled her off the ground, and swept her into the trees, fighting the pain-induced nausea the exertion caused. A wave of heat threw them both flat on their stomachs. Groaning in pain, Lairn rolled over and stared back at the deer trail.

Kiel screamed, engulfed in flames. The dragon, attracted to the scent of blood and having two sources to choose from

— the wound on Lairn's head and the soaked cloth in the wizard's pocket — had chosen the stationary target. Kiel had caught the full blast.

As Lairn watched in stunned horror, the dragon swooped low and plucked the burning wizard from the trail, flying back toward the mountain with him.

Smoke billowed around the trees, and Sayla began to cough. Lairn hauled himself to a sitting position to cradle her.

"Took...you...long enough," she gasped.

"I like to make an entrance," he said, smiling.

* * *

Sayla stood in front of the dragon, heart racing. Sweat trickled down her face, but she was afraid to raise her hand to wipe it away. Behind her, she could hear the river rushing past.

She tried to take a step to the side, but the dragon snorted twin puffs of steam and lowered its head in readiness to shoot flames. She froze, praying it would relax.

A month ago, one dragon nearly ate me, a wizard tried to kill me, Mother disowned me - again - when I told her I was leaving...I survived all that just to get roasted alive, she thought with a scowl.

A strong hand gripped her arm.

"You always choose the strangest places to wait for me, princess," Lairn said in her ear.

Relaxing and flashing him a smile, she allowed him to guide her as they backed away from the dragon. "At least I'm not drunk."

He chuckled, guiding her another step back. The dragon rumbled a warning.

"I owe you an apology," Lairn said.

"Now?"

"What better time?"

"What do you have to apologize for?"

"I'm sorry your father fell."

The dragon took a step toward them, glaring.

"He wouldn't have been up there in the first place if I hadn't run off," Sayla said. "How are we going to get away from this thing?"

"The river. If we can get to it, we can float down to the treeline and lose him in the woods." He gave her arm a gentle squeeze. "I'm sorry for everything that happened after your father died, too, Sayla. I should have been there for you, instead of worrying about the next fancy dress I was going to buy for you."

Sayla felt soft mud under her feet. Another step, and they would be in the water. She thought about the grief she'd gone through alone, the resentment she'd felt for Lairn, and the longing for home that had driven her from him in the end.

The dragon huffed, expelling the foul scent of sulfur.

"I'm sorry too," Sayla said. "I told Mother that I won't be going back." She stole a glance at his face, and grinned at the surprise in his expression.

He took a deep breath, turned, and gave her a quick kiss just before pulling her into the river.

Holding hands, they floated away, leaving the frustrated dragon to trumpet its fury on the riverbank.

Hell? or Naught?
ChaosInOrder

Why do I still think of you?
now that everyone has gone
though they've not been gone
as long
as you

Why is it your face I see?
as I free fall towards hell
because we walked in hell
so well
you see

and I need you now
I need a guide
I'm not sure
I don't think I can walk
the red hot path
I don't think I can walk
life's razor edge
alone

I know...I know
at times we did it badly
for years our lives churned madly
but it was fun
when two were one

but one is gone
what is left ?
subtract one
from one

the number that isn't
a man of naught
something that can never be
something only naught can see

0

Empty....in the western way
nothing even there
to decay
Nothing
leaves no mulch
Nothing cannot perpetuate
What cannot be known
cannot be grown
nor shown
because

0

(what you get when you take one from one)
is naught

Being Regular
K.A. Thompson

I spent $1.15 on a soda so small it could send a thirsty toddler into a major meltdown. And they call it a "tall," not "microscopic, two sips and you're done, small" as they probably should. The cup—and I just measured—is just a tad taller than my middle finger is long. And trust me, I have small hands.

Still, because I sit here in the café, taking up space, I felt compelled to buy the drink. It's not as if I don't really want it, I do; it's the idea of dropping over a dollar for less soda than I could get in a 25 cent can of WalMart's house brand (which, in my esteemed opinion, is pretty darned tasty.)

I'm not the only one. There were seven or eight other people in here, doing what I'm doing—pretending to work or study—and all purchased the obligatory cheapest menu item to feel justified in taking up space.

Somehow I doubt the bookstore police (oh, yeah…the café is in a bookstore) are going to storm in and beat us all about the head and shoulders with wet sweat socks if we wander in and sit down without buying anything. It's the principle of the matter: you take up a business's space, you buy at least a small part of their product.

I do this a lot. I wrote at least half of a novel sitting in this café (but hey, not all in one day…), and have taken notice of the regulars here. Many seem to be students of the university down the road, in search of a quiet place to study and work on class assignments. I've often felt the impulse (but never acted on it) to point out that the McDonalds just across the street from the school, is usually just as quiet, and a whole lot cheaper.

I know that because I wrote part of a novel there, too.

Come to think of it, of the three novels I've written, most of them were penned in McD's, the café, the food courts of Travis AFB and Wright Patterson AFB, Burger King, and Taco Bell.

There's a pattern there.

And it's evident: writing books contributes to weight gain.

But, the regulars.

Of all the regulars, the most visible is Douggy. I know his name only because some of the employees greet him with the same infectious enthusiasm that the regulars on *Cheers* greeted Norm. They gleefully call out his name, and instantly have ready for him his favorite beverage along with a cookie or brownie. They watch for him; when someone notices Douggy in the parking lot, it's a race to the door to let him in, and accompany him to the café where his favorite table, or one close to it, is cleaned off, and where he is served.

Douggy is most visible because he arrives via the county bus-taxi service in a large and brightly painted motorized wheelchair, and because he is carefully fed his cookie or brownie by the blonde girl who works behind the counter, as they carry on a conversation only she can really understand.

People stare, and whisper, as people are wont to do. Most of the regulars smile and wave their fingers when Douggy arrives, acknowledging him as one of us. A person and not a sideshow.

The day I inadvertently sat at Douggy's table, engrossed in my own work (or perhaps a game of computer *Scrabble*; it's hard to remember, but with my work ethic…it was probably *Scrabble*), no one said anything, but as the door to the bookstore was held open, my internal voice piped up, and I casually moved to another table.

Confetti did not pour from some hidden spot in the ceiling. No one cheered or offered me a bright and shiny mylar balloon for my consideration. My moving was expected; not required, but expected. Kind of like what anyone would do if they were perched upon Norm's *Cheers* stool. The courteous thing to do is move, without fanfare and without expectation.

There's another guy I see here quite often. He sits with his back to the window, holding a coffee cup between his hands, and watches people in the café. Well, he stares. And he doesn't seem to care that people not only realize he's staring at them, but it makes them uncomfortable. I tend to think of him as "Creepy Guy" (not to be confused with the old man at the YMCA pool who stares at me while I swim. He's "Creepy Old Guy.")

I'm not sure I've ever seen Creepy Guy take a sip from the coffee cup he holds possessively between his hands. As far as I can tell, he just buys the thing to have a reason to sit there and stare.

There's an older couple (older than me, in any case, and these days I'm quite happy to find people older than me out and about) who are here almost every time I am. They each buy a coffee and a freakishly huge cookie, then sit at a table for two, where they talk about their grandkids (perfect little angels, of course, even the one who whipped it out and peed on the fake tree at the mall food court), the trips they've taken (making me want to go see the World's Biggest Ball Of Twine, too), and their finances. That last one usually sparks a tense, teeth-clenched, under-the-breath argument about shoes she doesn't need, and tools he's too stupid to use correctly. As far as I can see, he hasn't yet cut a finger off, but she reminds him that he *did* sand a hole through one of the chairs that goes to her grandmother's antique dining set.

That shuts him up for a minute, and I'm pretty sure she's headed to the mall and every store that sells spiffy new shoes.

Often—though not as often as I see other people—there's this young woman (25 or thereabouts) who brings her young son; most of the time she has just bought him a new book, and he sits at the table, pretending he can read. His face is unusually serious for a three year old, but it's a seriousness borne of determination: he will read the entire text of *If You Give A Mouse A Cookie* before they leave. When he's done, he slams the book closed and proclaims "That's just not right."

I'm not sure what's not right. Mice do like cookies; I've seen one try to carry off an entire Oreo. And I'd think that if you *did* give a mouse a cookie, or a part thereof, you'd be obligated to follow through.

There's usually an odd assortment of FrankenWalkers, kids just learning to master their own feet, and quite often they're fascinated by what must be extremely new shoes. They walk with their heads down, staring at the contraptions Velcroed in place; I now understand this, having recently acquired a spiffy new pair of red, white, and blue Converse Chuck Taylor's. Yes, for the first day or so, I frequently watched my feet, enthralled by the canvas pseudo-flags sticking out from the bottom of my jeans.

Okay. Yes. I'm 42 years old. I bought shoes better suited to a 16 year old. But they're *spiffy*. They're *Chuck's*. And they match my brand new red, white, and blue leather flag jacket.

It's not a midlife crisis thing. Not even accounting for the fact that last year I bought a shiny red convertible. Nope.

Do I wonder what the other regulars think about the middle aged housewife who sits there with a notebook or sometimes a laptop computer, scribbling away, dressed like a backwards teenager?

Sometimes. But I'm fairly sure I'm not as interesting to them as they are to me. At least not on the days I'm not talking to myself.

Once in a while, kids (especially those who are there often) will walk up and ask what I'm doing (and as tempted as it is, I've never answered "writing porn, go ask Mommy what that is!") and start a conversation to the horror of their parents—parents who were paying such close attention that they failed to notice when their precious offspring wandered away.

Most of them are attracted by my jacket; that's my assumption, spurred on by a two year old who pointed at me and squealed "Fag!"

That's toddler-speak for "flag."

Right?

The thing about the regulars: while we acknowledge each other, we do not speak to each other. It's silent courtesy; we know we're not there to socialize for the most part. Some of us are there to write the next Great American Novel, some are there to scratch out the Perfect Term

Paper, some to unwind, to reconnect with the person on the other side of the same table, but we're not there to make friends. Any details we know about one another are discovered only through bits and pieces of overheard conversations.

Until today.

Douggy has not been seen in the café in over a week. His absence has been noticed, definitely, but people miss days here and there. Being at the café from 1-3 p.m. is not a requirement, and there is Real Life out there. So the first few days of Douggy's absences were noted, but not with concern.

But today Creepy Guy put his cup down on the table, and asked of no one in particular, "Where's Douggy?"

Everyone looked up from what they were doing and glanced at Douggy's vacant table. Not only was Douggy not there, but the blonde who always greeted him with an explosive smile and cookies, who patiently fed him and wiped his chin of crumbs and dribbles, always with the utmost care and respect, was also absent.

So today we talked, comparing mental notes. "When did you last see him?" "How was he? Looking tired? Happy? What?" "What about the girl? Anywhere around so we can ask her?"

We moved from our respective spots and sat together, wondering out loud where the kid with the bright grin and killer wheels was. As far as we could figure out, no one had seen him in at least a week. Neither had we seen the blonde girl.

Our loud conversation caught the ear of the other girl working behind the café counter; she set aside her towel and came over to us, pulling over a chair from another table.

The blonde is Douggy's sister.

And Douggy, who evidently refused to allow his disability to get the better of him, bravely driving his brightly painted wheelchair on even the busiest of streets, entered a crosswalk at precisely the moment the driver of a minivan chose to answer her cell phone.

She took her eyes off the road just long enough to miss the fact that the kid in the wheelchair had rolled off the sidewalk. Just long enough for her to plow into him at full speed. At 45 miles an hour.

Douggy never had a chance.

The silence that fell over the two tables we occupied was an uncomfortable pause of concern; in a movie it would have exploded like a spent bubble, anger demanding retribution, the driver of the minivan's head on a platter.

One by one we retreated to our former tables. And then one by one people left. Students went to their classes. The older couple headed out, and as he shoved his empty cup into the trash can he commented on the sale at shoe store just down the street. The café girl went back to work, cleaning the counter.

I looked at my too-expensive toddler soda, wondering what I should think. What I should feel. I did not know Douggy, not in the least. I do not know what caused him to live out his life in a motorized wheelchair, or even how long he had been in it. I never guessed that the blonde was his sister.

I never thought to ask.

I never presumed to strike up a conversation with Douggy or his sister. Or anyone else.

I'm here to work.

I come in here and pay too much money for too little drink, so I can work.

Creepy Guy pushed himself up with a loud sigh, crumpling the foam coffee cup in his hand. He paused before heading for the door, and looked at me. Not in my general direction, but at me, he looked into my eyes.

"I'll see ya around," he said. "Take care."

One Year

Tracy Crowe

I don't want to be
On the hurting
End of the stick
Anymore

But that sword
It cuts both ways
Cold

And bitterly cold
Will not melt
The ice
That has formed
A glass cage
Around my heart
Since he left me
In tatters and
A crying rage

The ache is softened
By the ticks
On the clock
But it feels
All over now
Like the pages
Have been turned
And cannot be
Unwritten

I cannot rewrite
  Your love
  Your part
In this play that
Flings itself
Across my stage

The fallen sparrow
Is a stone's throw away
And the universe
Made a hard turn
Into my heart

I see no hands
Reaching out
To guide me
In this shadowy land
But it's almost dark
And it's almost day

I say I don't want
What I cannot have

But the crying mask
Begins to break and
Crack
To fall to the
Floor
And a pea-sized
Bite of hope
Is glowing just
Underneath
The skin

I have eaten
The promise
I wait for it
To grow.

Blood of the Lamb
Stephen W. Cote

BROKEN WHEEL

The oldest dream always comes first: his brother attired in the turned-out cloak of an Arabian peasant, only his head and shoulders are visible. A scenic mountain vista halos his brother's crown so that the hues of spring soften his complexion into alcohol-blurred gold. For a moment, there is only raw and unfiltered peace pouring from his brother's eyes in unadulterated altruism for the object of his attention. The halo darkens and without pause a colorless mass blots out the visage of his brother's head. This dream frequents his restless sleep.

And by his namesake, Cain, he always arrived at the same conclusion as to the meaning.

But the most recent dream he knew to be true. Just as John Hardin was rising to his own prominence in Texas, he had already made a name for himself in his own way. No matter what historians may deduce, Cain was the last traveler to visit many settlements with the *Ghost Town* moniker. And his methods were brutal in their simplicity: kill every living creature.

Cain never remembered his brutality and only knew of his activities by the odd places he found himself and the murderous dreams haunting his slumber. He never stole anything, as if he prided himself in preserving at least one commandment. That is, unless murder qualified as breaking multiple commandments if one considered such acts a theft of life. Possessions, those he never stole.

Though he had no coherent memory of his actions, he found himself believing in them and even slipping into daydream-dialogues that circuitously supported those beliefs. He would ride his horse and his mind wandered with the rhythmic canter across a wind-tilled field.

He was having a heart-to-heart talk with Hardin, as though the two had been tight.

Before any words were exchanged, Hardin sauntered up to the bar where Cain was drowning-down the trail dust with whiskey; the trail was always dusty in spite of the weather. Cain reflected on Hardin's remark that he could have put a shot through his head before Cain had time to draw. Cain finished his whiskey and begged Hardin to cast his eyes down at his lap where his pistol was already drawn, cocked, and aimed upwards and towards Hardin's chin. Both men shared a hardy chuckle over the exchange and Cain bought Hardin a drink. After a brief exchange of pleasantries, the two men discussed their preferred methods for plying their barbarous trade. Cain made use of this time to impart his own wisdoms.

In an over-accentuated drawl, Cain said, "I've never had a showdown at high-noon, walked down the center of the town's main street, waited to draw, walked ten paces, or exchanged pithy dialogue. For example," he extrapolated, "I once poked my head inside a saloon and shot a bastard in his chair. Another time, I walked up and shot a cowpoke while he was chattering with his cowpoke crew."

"And posses?" Hardin asked.

Cain smiled, bemused. "Ambush 'em from behind and would shoot anyone who looks like they might talk." He flashed a broad smile, "Which, as it always turned out, tends to be everyone."

While the two conversed, and the drinks flowed, Hardin grew drunk and Cain detailed one of his most cherished accomplishments. "In eighteen seventy-two, I was the number one cause for the creation of Ghost Towns. But, there ain't nobody left to pin that particular medal."

Hardin raised a toast to Cain's accomplishments and bought another round.

In the depths of Cain's fantasy, Hardin seemed close to passing out and pushed himself away from the bar and retired to have a turn with Cookie Batter, or whatever the head-whore's name was.

With Hardin out of earshot, Cain felt more open to talking a little smack.

"The Earps are pansies, but I don't reckon they aren't able. Everyone thinks Hardin is the end-all-be-all bandit," and he glanced up towards the second floor of the bar. He fell silent and looked with a drunken gaze at the door Hardin had entered, belonging to Horse Radish Sue's room or whatever her name was. "But that's just it," he continued explaining to a non-confrontational cowpoke and the bartender, when he wasn't pouring drinks. "Hardin's a bandit. A marauder. A punk. Yes, he is a crack-shot, but then, aren't we all?. At this level," he gestured towards himself and also towards the door

Hardin had entered, "It's a matter of degree, too. I wouldn't try to shoot the pistol out of your hand at thirty paces. No," he said leaned closer towards his audience, "I'd shoot at your knees, maybe, then walk up and shoot your hands, and maybe shoot you in a few other painful places. Then, when you were bloodied and writhing," he envisioned several squirming gunfighters on the perennially dusty street, "I might even kill you."

"Jesse James," Cain said with a smile and smacked the 'M' in James. "Jesse got caught up in believing he was some kind of hero, but at first he admitted he was just a no-good thief and murderer. I suppose you could say I like the fellow for that honesty."

"Who do you admire?" A card-shuffling shopkeepers or shifty-eyed squatters asked him. He didn't see who asked. Normally, he would never admit it, but happened to be drunk enough at that moment. There is one man I think really identifies the era of history in which we live. And, that man is Jeremiah Johnson from Montana. Ol' Liver-Eatin' Johnson. A decent man, I suppose, until Indians up and killed his wife and daughter." Cain leveled his eyes at a squatter who was listening intently. "Yes sir, Jeremiah knew how to exact revenge, and he knew how to continually exact it over and over. I like to think that I live my life the same way that Johnson lived his. Figure out what really gets to the heart of humanity, and keep it up. Genocide works for me."

Cain drifted from the bar to the street where he encountered some young pup. He imparted his wisdom as though his audience begged for his words, flakes of heavenly manna, to fill their bellies through their ears.

A simple boy with saucer-wide eyes listened attentively. "I've never worn a cowpoke's sombrero," Cain said, flipping the brim of the boy's oversized hat, "or any hat at all unless the weather is so foul that Noah himself starts building another big canoe. And, I immediately remove my spurs when I dismount because they make too much ruckus and slow him down. I don't wear a pistol belt or stitch holsters to my clothes. Instead," he patted his trousers, "I keep them here, against my thighs, or sometimes against my chest. Keeps them from freezing-up, and folks aren't as jumpy if they don't see a man walking around with pistols. And," he said with a cautionary and booze-soaked tone, "I never drink whiskey, or smoke tobacco, or fornicate with prostitutes or women of lowly social status." He smiled and his chest swelled. "Have pride in yourself, boy, because that may be all you'll ever have in the world."

The boy muttered something about the local prostitutes, and Cain remarked, "In the past I've taken women by force when the time and place were suitable to my inclination. But, there are so many virtues that it's hard to remember all of them." The boy smiled and Cain elaborated. "I've never robbed a train, a bank, a stage-coach, or a cashbox, but sometimes I'll pick the pockets of someone I killed because it couldn't be stealing if they were already dead, right?"

"But," Cain warned, "if someone shoots at me, I'll shoot anyone and everyone else after I've done in the shooter because, the way I figure it, they'll might come for me next if they didn't have the decency to warn me. And, if someone warns me, well, I have to shoot them on principle because they could have just shot whoever who was aiming to shoot me in the first place."

So went his fantasy. He didn't know what was memory or dream because he didn't remember doing any of it, except one recent event.

Savannah Cline. Their love had been pure and complete. A love, she had said, whose bonds would only be broken in death. Cain had always assumed it would have been his death or hers, but apparently it applied to others' death as well. All he knew was that at one point they had traveled to Little Rapids, Wyoming, and, one night as he slept, she had left without a word. A year later, he returned to Little Rapids and found most of the townsfolk's possessions strewn about, but no townsfolk.

Cain didn't know what happened at Little Rapids, but his one memory of actually being in a gunfight involved Savannah Cline. They had stopped at a small mining town, taken a drink and some victuals at the shack decorated with a sign identifying it as the bar, and some lanky kid sauntered in. He reckoned Cain was the infamous gunfighter out of Texas, and Cain didn't consider at the time that perhaps the kid was confusing him with Hardin. The kid had an itchy trigger finger, everyone could tell, and when Cain brushed him off with a smart quip, the kid made an unflattering remark towards Savannah.

Cain knew the kid wanted to gun him down, and at that moment knew the kid would probably draw in Savannah's direction just to get him to draw. His mind had raced and his hands started to shake. His entire body palsied with epileptic reaction to everything around him and his senses became sharpened as though he might cut down the kid with a mere thought. Cain's pistol was in his hand and pointed at the kid as though the kid had become frozen in the preceding seconds. The kid had enough time to form a horrified expression, realizing he had made a mistake. Then Cain fired.

Tales of self-defense were good only in wholesome parlance because the stories usually involved no wrongdoing on his part and offered appropriately meted justice. Such stories reminded Cain of his oldest dream.

After Savannah left him, Cain tried to think about everything he could remember from Little Rapids and his own proclivity for gun-slinging, but couldn't fathom her reaction solely from those two potential causes. Then, he thought more about himself and his own daily habits and began to realize that, perhaps, he had a problem.

He did. Besides not remembering things he was apparently supposed to remember, he had a more functionally and obvious problem. He couldn't concentrate. The more he tried to think about why Savannah left him, the more he realized that he couldn't think about it because mere seconds passed before his mind began to wander. Then he would become angry without knowing why he was angry, or what he had been thinking about.

Whether it was a subconscious pursuit or happenstance, Cain had found himself in Liberty, Washington, a young mining town. There he remained for four years and, at some point and for a time, his problem was solved. In those peaceful years, he developed strong bonds with the Palouse tribes, and had found love. However, the tribes had not been receptive to the influx of settlers and soldiers, and animosity grew between the tribes, settlers and soldiers. Cain realized that the respite he had enjoyed in Liberty was ending.

Cain sat bareback on and astride Mescaline, an ornery Appaloosa, and he looked upon a valley from a craggy ridge. A Palouse tribe encampment dotted the Western bank of a narrow river that swung northeast to southwest through the valley. His pistol was in his hand and the muzzle thrust under a man's chin before the man's fingers had made contact with his shoulder. The man was sitting tall on his horse

A Clear Horizon

and Cain's pistol hand was raised at an awkward angle.

Cain had not heard a horse approach, but had reacted as though he knew someone was near.

The Palouse warrior's gaze was unblemished by fear and he slowly raised a small doeskin pouch.

Cain withdrew the pistol, tucked it under his shirt, and slowly took the pouch. He weighed it in his palm and looked forlornly at the formidable warrior. "So little," he remarked with a sad tone to his voice. He smiled gamely, then recognized the face and the trials both behind and before him. "John Bear," he said with a measured breath.

"My English name," the warrior replied stone-faced, behaving as though Cain's reaction was expected.

Cain guided Mescaline around to fully face the proud warrior. "And your real name," he said then paused, struggling to recall. He knew that if he ingested the contents of the pouch, a medicine, he would remember and he would once more enjoy a simple and wholesome life, the kind most people take for granted. The kind of life he had had in Liberty with a woman named Genevieve. Mescaline neighed and turned his head towards the pouch, nipping at Cain's fingers. His horse certainly knew what the contents were.

John Bear reined in his steed and pursed his lips. "In the years of our friendship, you could never pronounce it right. You always said something that translated as Outhouse Door or Stinky Place instead of Moon Tree, which is what you were always trying to say, but which still isn't accurate." He narrowed his eyes, "Not all tribal names translate into some conjunction of nature." A tight smile crossed his lips. "If you couldn't get it right when you were thinking clearly, you won't get it right now. John Bear will suffice."

Cain observed John Bear's stature as a soft wind bristled

the fringes of John Bear's long black hair. Glancing down at his pistol, and with fragments of his memories becoming more cohesive, he asked, "What goes through your mind when I draw my pistol? You had time to fire an arrow from a long ways back, or draw one of those knives in your belt, or even your own pistol. Why did I even get a chance to draw?"

John Bear pointed across the valley and in the direction of the breeze. Apparently, he had answered this particular question before given the way he rattled off his reply. "It is like looking at a strong wind. No matter your intent or convictions, the strong wind will avert your gaze. So is it with trying to raise an arm to you. It is as though the arm is simply pushed away with a force insurmountable by the strength of the arm."

"I always thought I was just fast," Cain admitted sullenly.

"Do not confuse your abilities with the inequities of others," John Bear mentored. "You have an uncanny ability in your trade. There is also some other spirit that fights alongside you."

"Your English has certainly improved," Cain quipped. He then realized he recalled a time when John Bear's English wasn't spoken so well. "I guess I've already told you that."

Looking at John Bear, Cain recollected why his English was well spoken. Cain had taught him over the previous four years, and John Bear had spent time scouting and acting as liaison to the Nez Perce for the Union troops garrisoned in Spokane and Walla Walla.

"Colonel Wright's troops are now holding Liberty," John Bear said in a wounded tone, changing the subject, "and it is becoming clear to us that the Palouse tribes will be overrun, just as the Nez Perce is being overrun and just as the other tribes on the far side of the land have been overrun." John Bear looked out over the valley and fell silent, then removed two knives from his belt and offered them to Cain.

Cain took both and looked at them, one large and one small. "One is for Genevieve," he said to himself and then remembered that in Genevieve he again had found the kind of love he had experienced with Savannah.

John Bear nodded brusquely. His eyes were affixed to Cain's and he said, "It pains me to see you suffer as you had before, and I am," he paused then, visibly grief-stricken and searching for the right words, "I am ailing, but I am pleased that you will honor the bonds of our friendship in exacting vengeance in the name of our people."

Before Cain could remark upon his uncertainty, John Bear continued, "You will understand when you take the medicine."

"Now," John Bear said and his eyes were misted-over, "I must ride out with my people who even now make haste to give you a wide berth."

"Thank you," Cain said weakly, then added with an affection that he hadn't been aware that he felt, "my friend."

"And don't give any to your horse," John Bear said as he spun his mount away from Cain and began to ride away.

ROAD TO LIBERTY

How that winter wind howls o'er the Palouse. The pungent aroma of cattle dung was whipped into the stinging breeze giving the evening air a distinct bite. Snow gusted instead of falling and was little more than sandy granules of ice that were blown into every crevice of fabric. The medicine John

Bear delivered brought clarity to Cain's thoughts, sharpening his intellect but strangely dulling his instincts. He felt sluggish, even in the loose fitting winter cloak a Nez Perce woman had presented him some years past.

Genevieve Rauessou's pony, Black Grama, was a spotty little mare, not quite old or pokey enough to be overly slow, and who seemed to take great pride in antagonizing Mescaline. Genevieve had been handling the winter ride in that fertile and hilly land well, though kept to her fashions by wearing one of her thick French-made outfits. The fabric was felt dyed in Indigo and trimmed with thick white fox fur. Though ill suited for riding and already soiled about the breaches, it was undoubtedly warm.

With evening setting upon them, Cain brought Mescaline to a halt in a small river valley, dismounted, and then assisted Genevieve down from Black Grama. When she reached the ground, she threw her arms around his shoulders and gave him a great hug.

"How are you doing?" she asked, her mouth slightly aquiver and shrouded in a billow of condensation.

Cain nodded and started shuffling around through the snow, looking for loose wood. He found a few large branches and went about making a fire. He fetched a tinderbox from one of the saddlebags strapped to Mescaline and crouched near the pile of sticks and branches. While he was collecting wood, Genevieve had unpacked two thick hides and two blankets. She then crouched near him and put her slender arm, clad in designer fabrics, around his shoulder.

"Are you alright?" she asked again, the rich texture of her French accent adding ambient warmth.

Cain nodded again, chipping at the flint over a small bit of kindling. "I'm cold, especially my head" he said with an uncharacteristic drawl, and patted his mostly bald head.

"I think you're the only man I've met this side of the country who won't wear a hat." She wrapped one of the blankets around his shoulders, and then was silent until the kindling was lit. As the glow of the fire brightened enough so that she could see his long and gaunt face, she asked more quietly, "You're feeling well, though? It's been so nice these last few days, even in such forbidding weather."

"It has been," he agreed sullenly, pulling the blanket across his arms. "But there wasn't much medicine this time and I can already feel it wearing off."

Genevieve looked to the far side of the fire and away from Cain. "The tribe hasn't moved that far away yet. I'll have to ride out in a day or two if I am to meet up with them." She glanced at Cain from the corner of her eyes, gauging his reaction.

He put his arm around her and leaned away from the growing fire. "I have to do this."

Genevieve shook her head and touched her hand to his face. "No, you don't," she said softly though with an earnest tone. "We can ride further west, or go to Montana."

Cain smirked and shook his head. "I can't go back there."

"I don't believe that," she said. "For all these years I've known you, you've never acted like you talk. Now you are riding to Liberty and I'll never see you again." She raised her hands in a gesture of helplessness and despair, admitting, "I can't see you again"

Cain looked at her with a hurt expression. "Have a little faith in me. I may not die."

She closed her eyes and pulled away from his loose embrace. "How I have come to love you, but I cannot be with you if you design to take life. And it's all over a matter of horses."

"Wright ordered the slaughter of eight hundred horses," Cain said with a measured voice. "They were the lifeblood of the tribe. And they have done far worse than that. The tribe beseeched repayment for this debt, and its name is vengeance."

"And the settlers they killed for no reason? The scouts that were ambushed when they posed no threat? It seems to me that although we made our trespasses, they were killing or robbing from those explorers and settlers from the start." Genevieve shook her head. "I just don't see where you owe them this debt."

She removed a small knife from her pocket, the same knife Cain had passed on to her from John Bear. The craftsmanship was exquisite, and when she unsheathed the blade the polished metal gleamed in the growing fire. A blackened horse was engraved on the flat of the blade and a branch bearing her likeness graced the opposite side. "Who am I to receive such tokens? A knife so that I might cut away my own heart when I can no longer live without you at my side?" She shook her head. "They mistook that weakness because I won't pine for you when you've forced my hand to ride away."

Cain withdrew the knife John Bear gave him and held it next to hers. "It is for safe passage through other tribes. Not because they thought you to be weak, but because they knew you had to make this sacrifice. You are compelled to leave just as I am compelled to continue."

"And the medicine?" Cain then asked. "I don't fully remember the first time we met, except that you had told me I had struck you as a man of ill repute."

Genevieve set her knife in her lap and took hold of Cain's hand still wielding his sheathed knife. "I ask you what debt is so great that you burden yourself with a task that is not so bold or daring but murderous and foolhardy? I stayed with you in Liberty, and I stayed with you these last years with the tribe because I understood their ways as genteel, even if outwardly all others saw them as barbarous. Just as I condemn Colonel Wright for being so rash, so do I hold the tribe, and you Cain, to account for their reaction, whatever it may be. In those tender moments we had and hardships we shared with the tribe, we gave back what we took."

She gently took the knife from Cain's hand and set it upon the ground. "What goods or graces have we taken without repayment?" She tilted her head towards the horses, "a crazy horse named for the medicine they gave you and an old nag named for that rancid feed the horses get this time of year. A couple knives whose blades were machined, and spotty engravings that could be anyone? I do have good will for their countenance and graces, but we owe them nothing."

"I'm not saying they haven't been good to us," she continued, becoming more exasperated. "Everyone speaks or thinks as though you are some terror who slaughters entire towns and garrisons of soldiers, but I just don't see that in you."

Genevieve shook her head sadly. "I suppose the real pain I feel is that you can collect your thoughts enough to show your love and commitment to the tribes, but need medicine to love me."

"No," Cain said after considering what Genevieve had spoken. He in turn took both of her hands into his. "Their medicine has been the only thing I've found that makes me see the world like everyone else. With the medicine gone, I don't rightly know how I'll make it to Liberty; though I couldn't make it at all if I use the medicine." He moved one pair of clasped hands to the center of his chest. "I have a feeling that this is something I need to do precisely because I wish to honor my debt."

Debt. Cain considered the word as it weighed heavy upon his mind to hear Genevieve's repeated claim that he had none. He didn't believe that. Cain felt that all he had was debt for which there was no true absolution. Yet, he couldn't explain or understand what compelled him to make decisions that served no cause but to incur further debt. On the matter of Liberty, he thought that if he could carry out this one commitment he would at least repay one debt even if he incurred another.

"If I could explain my need to act, and describe what compels me to honor their request, then I wouldn't need the medicine and we could ride off together and forget this cold place. But I have memories and dreams that feel old and worn-out, and feelings that are both fatigued and indescribable. My love for you, this love we have now and have shared, is fresh and wholesome. But, beneath that love are actions I may or may not have taken, well before meeting you or the tribe, and if I have no debts to the tribe then I certainly have debts for my other trespasses. Real, or only imagined, I can't escape its madness, only temporarily put it to rest with the medicine. If going to Liberty will halt these thoughts and visions, then I must go." He paused and looked upon her with a forlorn gaze.

Cain leaned in to Genevieve and kissed her winter-chilled lips very lightly, and said, "It is because I love you, and because I want to be with you, that I must go to Liberty. If I don't, and with no further medicine, I fear I will once more be a man with whom you would not associate."

"Then given a choice between me and death, you choose death." She looked down at her lap.

"I choose you," Cain said, struggling to clarify his

argument in his own head. "Death isn't a choice. But, neither is it something that can be avoided."

"And you're riding out to meet it." She said acidly.

But Genevieve had discussed this with Cain before, and knew he could not be swayed from his course of action. In the morning, before the sun had risen and while Cain still slept, she would leave him and most likely never see him again. She loved him, but knew she could not be with him.

"Let's just enjoy these few hours we have," she whispered and the two lay down in the furs near the fire.

"I love you," Cain whispered to Genevieve later that evening, just before he went to sleep.

HIGH NOON

Where did she go? Why did Genevieve leave him? Cain awoke one morning to the discovery that she was no longer asleep by his side. He had vague recollections of being in Liberty before, and recalled that he had spent some time with one of the local tribes. Savannah Kline, and now Genevieve Rauessou. Both had ceased to be a part of his life.

Liberty. It had been a young mining town, at least so he recalled. The town was empty of life, nary a soul to be found, though he did remember a time when prosperity was whispered in the air and the bustle of growth echoed across the plains. He stood in the middle of the main street and wondered why he was there.

A heavy and dry snow had fallen over the previous days, and the entire town and surrounding valley and hills had a pristine countenance. The sky was a rich blue textured with fleeting wisps of clouds. The sun was directly overhead and its rays rained pleasant warmth on his balding and shorn head.

Liberty itself was small, but its construction was new. The porch boards didn't creak and some of the buildings still smelled like fresh-cut lumber.

Cain tethered Mescaline to a hitching post at the end of town, and walked to one of the buildings that seemed familiar. He glanced upwards at a picture window on the second floor and recalled a distinct memory of Genevieve looking down at him. A memory of being in the same room with her. Memories of intimate and clear-minded moments. Then, a sound caught his attention and the memories left his mind.

The sound of a single spur wheel being spun echoed throughout the town and Cain wheeled around, looking for the source. At the other side of the town, a man stood holding a spur.

Cain walked towards him, trying to gauge his intent but expecting the worst.

"Hell of a thing you did with those spurs back there," the man said.

Cain had no memory or recollected dream that specifically involved spurs, so said nothing.

"Half of a twenty-strong company clubbed before they even saw what happened, thinking you were just walking around the perimeter of their camp." The man spun the spur again and whistled. "You can pull out your pistol now if you think," but the man paused when he saw Cain had already moved.

Cain's torso palsied, and his already sharpened senses felt even more acute and taut. His pistol was in his hand, the hammer cocked, and the trigger pulled halfway when he stopped. He recalled John Bear's description of the wind forcing him to avert his gaze, and so was it with his pistol. His finger was at the apex of its motion but yielded to an unseen wind. A spirit, as John Bear had said. A spirit that held his finger fast. The man dropped the spur and started walking towards him.

"Go ahead," he called, his voice brash and cocksure. "Shoot." He held out his arms, making himself a larger target.

Cain held the pistol aimed at the man's torso, but found himself brought to a pause. He didn't know why he paused, and his finger felt frozen inside the trigger guard, unable to move any further. After trying unsuccessfully for some time, he slowly lowered the pistol.

"Who are you?" Cain asked.

The man walked closer and then stopped when he was within an arm's length. "The Marshall," he answered simply.

"Marshall of what?" Cain asked and looked around. "The town is deserted."

The man shook his head with a crooked smile, "Not the Marshall of this or any town." He looked around him in a coy act of discovery as though he had just noticed the missing residents when Cain drew attention to the fact. "Yes, it appears that it is," the man said, then went on to explain, "Folks get a little edgy when a murderous devil is heading their way."

"I 'spect you're Colonel Wright, then? Come to tell the town to clear out because I was coming to make due for what you did to those natives?" Cain looked over the man then returned his pistol to his belt, under his shirt. He felt unsteady and nervous from being unable to fire the pistol, but managed keep his surprise under check since the man had not drawn his pistol.

"Interesting premise," the man said, amused, "but I'm not a soldier, and have played no part in these forays." He shook his head and chuckled, "Your woman was right. This was a misguided effort at justice, Cain, and no good can come from it. Genevieve, was it? French whore you picked up from some mining town?"

Cain held his breath, observing the man. He seemed privy to his conversations and knew his name, intimating that he had either spied on him or somehow had gotten to Genevieve. That, and he didn't want to believe it but had to consider that Genevieve told him. "You know my name," he tested. "And who are you to say someone like her was a ever a whore?" The concept of Genevieve in that line of work unnerved him, but it did not feel entirely false.

"We've met before, you and I." the man said and paused for his words to settle with Cain. "Consider what business a fair-looking lass has in the wilderness. Until she met you, she had no man, and this is not the time or place for the likes of her to act with the requisite independence."

Cain took a few steps to the side of the man, observing him. "I don't recall meeting you before today. I don't recollect your name. I don't think Genevieve would have told you any of this, whether of her own free will or under duress. And I certainly don't remember anything to do with the killing of any soldiers as you described. Who are you? What kind of hand are you trying to play here?"

The man nodded to either side of him, and only then did Cain see the other men. Twelve of them; six men lined up on either side of the street. They were dressed in heavy black winter coats and wide-brimmed hats, were clean-shaven, and looked upon Cain with haunted expressions. Each held long rifles and their coats were open to expose their pistol belts. None wore a badge, nor did the self-described Marshall.

"A trap!" Cain hissed. He had both pistols in his hands before anyone could react, both aimed at the Marshall. By

sheer will he forced his fingers upon both triggers and un-
loaded three rounds from each pistol before he could see any
reaction from the other men. As the cartridge-smoke cleared
from before his eyes, he could see nothing had changed at
all.

He expected them to draw and gun him down, but they
had not reacted. Their rifles remained in their arms and though
some had looked to see a reaction from the Marshall, the
others remained still. Although Cain fired a total of six times
directly at the Marshall's chest, he could not see that his bul-
lets struck his target.

Standing four paces away, the Marshall called out as
though Cain was on the far side of town, "You can't kill me,
Cain!" He walked closer and lowered himself so that one of
Cain's drawn pistols was pointed at his forehead. In a softer
tone, he said, "Not even like this."

Anger surged through Cain's body and he fired the pistol against the Marshall's head. Nothing. A bullet had been
fired but struck nothing. He looked at the other men and felt
uncertainty and fear bear down on him. His arms and hands
continued to palsy as they always had in a gunfight, but the
tremors had become so bad that he could no longer hold the
pistols and he dropped them to the ground. His eyes misted
over as his mind personified the specter of Death and fear
into this man standing before him.

The Marshall straightened himself and instinctively
touched his forehead, but he found no wound with his finger-
tips. He showed no sign of feeling any pain, nor did he feel
pain. "A paradox," he said.

"A what?" Cain asked weakly. His head felt light and
his arms and torso fatigued.

"You can't kill me, nor I you." The Marshall said, and

then nodded to the other men, and when Cain looked up again they had moved out of sight, but he couldn't ascertain where.

"They were just for effect," The Marshall admitted with a wry smile.

"Are you," Cain started to ask, searching for some explanation. Only one concept entered into mind. "The Devil?"

"Interesting question, however absurd in its irony," the Marshall said with a choked-off laugh.

Cain's weakness drove him to his knees and he pounded his fists into the snowy ground. "Then what are you?" Cain demanded.

"The question isn't who or what I am, Cain, but who are you?" The Marshall took obvious pleasure from the tortured conversation.

The Marshall approached Cain and looked down upon him. "Do you believe in the Bible, Cain? In God and in Christ?"

Cain found that he could only listen, having given no real consideration to such nonsense apart from drawing comparisons between his dreams and Biblical stories he had heard.

"How about Buddha, or Mohammed?" The Marshall continued. "Even if you don't, there is an interesting correlation between all of these purportedly religious traditions. Do you know what it is?"

"God is all of them?" Cain managed to reply.

The Marshall shook his head. "No. Each culture has it's own interpretation of a god, or multiple gods, or lack of a god, or a messiah. What they do have in common is some kind of a beginning, and at least the general concept that some group's or some individual's actions originated and preceded the need for the dictates of those beliefs."

He extended his hand to Cain. Cain looked at it carefully then accepted it, and the man helped him to his feet.

"I'm a Holy Trinity fellow myself," the Marshall said with some degree of pride. "In that context, consider the Ten Commandments, and particularly the sixth. Thou shalt not kill. Now, any reasonable man would consider that this commandment would not be necessary unless indiscriminate killing, or murder, was not already a problem. And, someone, somewhere in time, was the first. Now, by my set of beliefs," The Marshall paused when Cain spoke.

"You're talking about Cain and Abel," Cain said guardedly, not exactly sure what the Marshall was intimating.

The Marshall nodded. "Are you beginning to understand?"

"You're suggesting I'm like Cain?" Cain offered.

"Not like," The Marshall corrected.

"Then what?" he demanded.

"By my codex, you are at once a palpable and pungent sin of man, and the resolute proof that redemption is possible. The essence of your blood poured from Christ's Grail, for as it was his blood imparted unto man, so was it your blood, in part, his was deemed to cleanse. You are the crucible in which redemption is forged." The Marshall looked evenly at Cain.

"You expect me to believe in such stories?" Cain asked, now recovering more of his strength and growing angry again at such fairy tales.

Then, Cain was brought to silence when he realized the Marshall had drawn his pistol and had it aimed at his forehead. The Marshall moved so fast and surreptitiously that Cain had not seen him move at all.

The hammer on the Marshall's pistol was cocked and his finger firmly fixed on the trigger. The slightest nervous twitch would send the hammer falling onto the primer that would ignite the cartridge and send the bullet through Cain's head. Perhaps this was the moment he was expecting and waiting for. He was not afraid or even surprised, and could see the threshold between life and death before him. Inches away. And it wasn't so nearly terrible as he had imagined.

"It is not a question of belief, Cain," The Marshall said. "Not on your part, anyway. You are too much of a part of this world and a portion of this world's beliefs for your own doubts to matter. No, it isn't what you believe, but what others believe you to represent." He rotated the pistol very slightly so that Cain's attention returned to the barrel. "The only belief with which you need concern yourself is whether or not I am capable of killing you."

"You said you couldn't kill me," Cain tested. He judged whether or not he could pull his pistol and shoot the Marshall before the Marshall shot him, but his previously failed attempt was still burned in memory.

"I think you need to see it," The Marshall said, and pulled the trigger. The hammer fell. The cartridge ignited. The pistol fired mere inches from Cain's forehead.

"No!" Cain cried and moved to cover his head, to move away from the pistol. But it was too late and he realized he would die. Except there was no pain and no feeling other than the sensation of hot gas expelled across his face. He rubbed the sulfuric smoke from his eyes and looked anxiously at the Marshall.

The Marshall turned his pistol and fired it at one of the buildings. Wood splintered and the sound of gunfire rang throughout the town of Liberty. "I was permitted to pull this trigger, but I am not permitted to kill you, Cain. No one is."

"Why not?" Cain begged the question.

"Jesus! Read your Bible, for Christ's sake!" The Marshall

swore, apparently not concerned with incurring the ire of the very deities he claimed to believe in. "Hasn't anyone ever told you what it is like to try?"

"John Bear," Cain admitted. "He said it was like a wind that forces you to look away."

"It is no wind, but the wrath of God coming down upon you!" The Marshall said forcefully. "And such force is more terrible than the horror of any individual. It is one of the oldest and one of the only intractable pacts God made. Actually," he pulled his pistol again and held it for a moment in Cain's direction. "It must be a rather significant annoyance to Him to have his wrath evoked every time someone tries."

"Why try?" Cain asked cautiously. "You seem to take some small and disrespectful pleasure doing so."

"I said I believed," The Marshall said, "I didn't say I was necessarily his agent."

"Then," Cain started but was cut off when the Marshall shook his head.

"It's not so black and white that if I am not in league with good that I must be in league with evil. My purpose in such maddening chaos is less distinct than your own. My presence isn't noteworthy or mentioned at all in any surviving texts." The Marshall said.

"If I am, for the moment, to believe what you have said, then why are you here talking to me?"

The Marshall spread his arms wide and moved his hands to indicate the entire town. "All of this. You were far too comfortable and ineffective living with those Indians. Your role, whether you believe it or not, is one of chaos, disorder, and destruction. I was to bring you here and, with a few well-placed rumors, your reputation preceded you. Especially after the business with the soldiers and the spurs, no one was going to wait around for you to show up. Liberty is dead, and you killed it. The townsfolk are spread out around you, struggling towards some other hospice. Most of them won't make it in this weather. The women and children will collapse, the beasts will falter, then men will expel their last breaths."

The Marshall looked around the town, seeming pleased with what he saw.

Cain looked in the same direction, buts saw nothing but an empty town and snow covered ground. "I told you I had nothing to do with those soldiers!" Cain stated. "You cannot put such accusation and blame upon my shoulders."

"Even now you have no memory of events that happened so recently." The Marshall shook his head sadly, looking at Cain as though one might look upon a child's ignorance.

"Cain," he explained, "There are people in this world without reason, voice, or form. You can see them, hear them, and suffer their presence and actions, but they have no concept of attrition. They evoke vocal understanding without tacit committal. They have no ability to form an intrinsic belief in concepts such as a higher deity, or in more simple things such as love. Most people of this world, no matter the religion, live such lives and it is then believable that only the tiniest fraction of the whole world could possibly find redemption and a higher existence because the rest simply do not exist as more than animals with a familiar form." The Marshall narrowed his eyes and raised his finger, pointing at Cain.

"The moment the Biblical Cain fell from grace, he forgot that there was a higher existence that is attainable in this life." His voice became more like a preacher's as he said, "Love thy neighbor. Can you conceive of how hard that is? How many people feign love and friendship but have no actual belief or concept in what they profess to offer? How fast most people will turn their backs on you and take advantage of you, no matter how close you believe them to be? How easy it is for them to react with a pistol than it is for them to embrace forgiveness?"

"If you think of me as Cain from the Bible, are you suggesting I'm incapable of love? That I am one of these people you describe?" Cain asked with an annoyed tone. "The very love I had for Savannah and Genevieve, you're suggesting that wasn't real?"

"The gun fighter claims to attempting love for his neighbor prior to drawing his gun?" The Marshall mused with a calm grin. "The only faculty most people possess, including you, is the ability to lie to themselves."

Cain refused to believe him, and shook his head. "I may have trouble remembering some events, but I remember that I loved them."

"Cain," The Marshall said, "The very wrath of God is in your wake, and both Savannah and Genevieve, and might I add it strange that you happened to fall in love with two whores and probably equate the act of copulation with love, both of them could see it. Whores they may be, but they were capable of belief. Even thought they couldn't have guessed who you really were, deep down they knew they couldn't be around you."

Cain picked up his pistols from the snowy ground, tucked them in his belt, and faced the Marshall. "You never really told me why you are here." He held up his hand when the Marshall started to answer. "I mean why are you telling me this if I will only forget it?" He paused, furrowing his brow. "I cannot deny that it is strange I didn't kill you, or you I. Nor can I deny that I really am not sure where I have been since, without the medicine, my mind is not entirely clear. What I don't understand is why you are explaining this to me."

"Because it was necessary to stop you here in Liberty. Where would you go from here? You can't really return to your Indian friends since you didn't actually finish what you set out to do. You never even started. Yet, most of the town is dead because you were riding in, except that won't matter to your friends. You can't return to Genevieve, and I think we covered why not. You really have nowhere else to go except to stay here for a while." The Marshall looked around at the town. "Not bad. You might even get some company in a few months."

"You want me to stay? Why would I do that?" Cain asked, perturbed that this man would suggest he take lodging in a deserted town for no particular reason.

"If you leave now, you will find no sanctuary. The very fact that you travel further through this land you will leave God's wrath in your wake. Your Indian friends will lose their homes and lives to the settlers and soldiers. If you stay here, it could be different." A slight smile crossed the Marshall's lips.

"You set this up," Cain said slowly. "I still don't believe that I killed those soldiers, or any of your banter about me being some sub-human incapable of love. Whore or not, I love Genevieve. You may know what we said; you could have sent someone to spy on us. But you don't know what I think or who I love, so don't presume otherwise."

The Marshall shrugged but held his tongue when Cain raised his hand.

"I have another choice than staying in this abandoned town, or leaving." Cain removed his pistols from his belt and dropped them onto the ground, and then dropped the extra cartridges as well. "I may have done questionable things in my life, but I am not going to accept responsibility for every wrong committed in this world, and to suggest I am responsible for such a degree of hate and evil is just asinine."

Cain shook his head in disbelief and slowly backed away from the Marshall, moving towards Mescaline.

The Marshall raised his hands and smiled, holding a calm composure. "Cain, did you not believe me when I told you that the townsfolk were dead or dying?"

Cain continued to back away. "I'm not sure I believe anything that has transpired here, and certainly not any words I might hear from you lips."

"Even Thomas believed what he saw." The Marshall took several steps towards a building adorned with elaborate signage identifying it as a mercantile. He crouched, clutched a handful of snow, and he held the snow up and asked, "Do you not see the death you have wrought?"

"Snow," Cain said evenly and with complete sincerity. "What I don't see are your innuendos and metaphors." He stopped backing away and grew exasperated. "A bunch of snow isn't anything more than snow."

The Marshall's expression changed and he brushed his fingers through the flakes of snow in his hand. "Cain," he said in a softer albeit dispassionate tone, "This is the blood you have spilled." The Marshall did seem more curious about Cain's behavior than he had earlier.

Cain angrily kicked the ground with his left foot, then bent and snatched a handful of snow in his right and threw the loosely packed snow at the Marshall. "It's snow! There ain't nothin' in this town but you, me, and snow."

Cain started to back away again.

"No, Cain," The Marshall said. "You would deny your accomplishments just as you have denied your very nature?"

He brushed his hand on his trouser leg, clearing the snow from his palm, then held his hand up again. "No, it's not snow. It is the blood of innocence that seeps into this ground. It is the blood of your sacrificial lamb." A mild and bemused smile crossed his lips.

The Marshall walked towards Cain, who still backed away but let the Marshall close the distance between them. When he was within reach, the Marshall extended the hand that had held the snow and touched Cain's hand.

Cain pulled his hand away.

"The blood you spilled is on your hand." The Marshall looked thoughtfully at Cain and then around the town. "What a waste that you will not acknowledge your efforts. You have changed since the last time we met."

"I don't know you," Cain seethed and turned away. He walked briskly towards Mescaline, mounted him, and guided the horse directly away from the Marshall. Mescaline cantered away from the Marshall, and away from Liberty.

The Marshall called out, "Accept that a sacrifice was made. You've slaughtered your lamb. Will you not look?"

But Cain ignored him. He wasn't sure who the Marshall was, or what the Marshall was ultimately trying to do, but knew that the man's words had started to have an effect. Each time the Marshall called the snow blood, he started imagining that it was blood. He had started to see only red ground, and imagined that the townsfolk had not fled but lay at his feet in morbid repose. Cain chose not to hear those insane words.

Riding out of Liberty and in pursuit of Genevieve, Cain noticed a dark red smear on his hand where the Marshall had touched him. He looked at both hands but didn't see a cut. He imagined that it was only dirt, and coaxed Mescaline onwards.

From The Chaos Chair
ChaosInOrder

Sunflower amphetamine
Buddha looks up at the muse
Dalai lama headphones
the anger is a ruse

Pine needle dystopia
Ginsberg dances at her side
Edward Gorey notebook sky
no place left to hide

Deficit of disorder within
disc drive holds sweet Miss Martins smile
Wesley Crusher nom de plume
barefoot all the while

leaf tobacco bouncy ball
she smiles at what she sees
Dylan Springsteen paradox
brings her to her knees

futon soy milk calls to me
the muse says, "one more line"
mirthful glaring, black and white
obliged…now sleep till 9

Hit Man
Angie Mansfield

"Oh, shit," was the first thing out of her mouth when she opened the door.

I didn't take it personal; most people react like that when I pay them a visit. At least she wasn't shooting at me – yet. I fought down a queasy feeling brought on by travel sickness and continued.

"You know why I'm here, Mrs. Lake. Where is he?"

She responded with a stream of colorful expletives, some even I hadn't heard. I let her blow off some steam, until I got tired of standing in the horizontal rain. She turned away to push the door closed. I pulled my gun and gave her a little rap on the temple, enough to shut her up for a few minutes, caught her as she crumpled, and stepped inside. I laid her on the bench by the door – I'm a gentleman, whatever she may have thought of me.

She had the heat cranked up as high as it would go. I turned the thermostat down; already my jacket felt heavy on my back.

I knew the layout of the house from the drawings I'd been shown, but I took a good look around, anyway. I like to know where my exits are in case I need to make a hasty one, and pictures never do a house justice. This was a pretty nice place. Well-oiled hardwood floors; a huge, expensive-looking rug under the designer sofa in the living room; high-quality reproductions of some famous paintings.

Or maybe they weren't reproductions. Our boy was a wealthy man by less than legal means, and couldn't show it off outside without drawing unwanted attention. So he filled his house instead. Could be the little lady had a taste for high-dollar art.

The house reminded me of the life and home I'd had before this job, and a wave of homesickness washed over me.

Movement down the hall to the kitchen snapped me back to the present. I turned and dropped into a crouch, gun at the ready. But whatever had been moving down there was gone now. My turn to utter some expletives, though mine were mostly under my breath. A quiet beep from the pocket of my jacket warned me that the movement had not been a product of travel sickness-induced imagination.

I couldn't check out the kitchen with Mrs. Lake lying on the bench. She only had a little konk on the head and could wake up any time. I cursed for the whole minute it took me to tie her hands and feet and duct-tape her mouth. I crammed her into the already-crammed closet next to the front door, pulled out the gun I'd re-holstered, and started my search.

Now, a lot of guys in my line of work are cool as frozen yogurt, love their jobs, go through searches like this all gung-ho and macho. I never liked this part of the job. I'm not cool, and I don't fool myself into thinking so. By this point, I could feel the sweat running down my sides and my shirt sticking to my back. I would have loved to take off the jacket, but there was no guarantee I'd be able to come back for it. And, damn it, I liked that jacket.

So I sweated all the way down the hall, checking the

two rooms to my left as I went. Nothing in them but a study full of books that likely hadn't ever been cracked and a small den. It wasn't more than five minutes after the movement that I found myself in front of the kitchen doorway. Sweating like a hog standing in front of the butcher's block. On a hot day. Wearing a jacket.

I listened to the silent house for thirty seconds or so, but the only sounds came from the street and the rain splatting against the windows. Steeling myself and taking a deep breath, I burst through the door, covering first the right side of the room, then the other, expecting a bullet in the leg or back or head any second.

Nobody.

Empty kitchen, black refrigerator, black stove, black microwave. Dark oak cabinets, black marble counter tops. I eased around the center island, which had a plate and sandwich fixings on its polished black top. Bologna on rye. Extra mayo. Blech.

A glass sliding door led from the deserted kitchen to the back yard. The door was wide open, and a puddle was forming as a playful wind batted raindrops onto the granite tile floor. Wind felt like heaven on my overheated face as I surveyed the yard. No use chasing after him; he knew I was here. He'd be blocks away by now, and the rain would cause too much interference to scan for him. With a sigh, I closed and locked the door and headed back down the hall toward the stairs. I knew I'd find nothing on the second floor, and I started preparing myself for the next step.

Mrs. Lake was by all accounts a bitch, but I still hated questioning reluctant spouses and family. Sometimes the money didn't seem worth it. Shooting someone who was a confirmed thief, murderer, and all-around bad guy was one thing, but extracting information through pain wasn't my cup of tea.

I checked upstairs but, just as I'd thought, nothing and no one up there. I could feel my breakfast churning as I walked back down the steps toward Mrs. Lake's closet.

* * *

I am not a bad guy. I love puppies, adore children, and have a passion for gardening. I could be your next-door neighbor, your kid's soccer coach, or the guy who sells you your next car.

Okay, maybe not the guy who sells you a car. I'm trying, after all, to paint a *good* image here.

My chosen profession does not reflect the values that govern my home life. Does anyone's? I was...nudged toward the job by events beyond my control. I look back on things I've done and cringe as much as you no doubt will as you read the rest of my little tell-all. That does not, of course, absolve me of the sins I've committed.

Perhaps nothing can.

* * *

I left Mrs. Lake curled around her pain and fear much later than I'd hoped. In the end, I begged her to give me the information I sought, so I could get the nasty part of the business over quickly.

Some people don't understand that loyalty can be a liability.

The rain had stopped, and dying sunlight turned the water-laden trees amber, prematurely aging them into autumn's somber hues.

Or perhaps they seemed somber only because of the mood I was in.

Taking up the slack for my otherwise occupied mind,

my feet found their way to the small copse of trees at the edge of the subdivision, where I'd ported in earlier. People in this time weren't ready to see a hulking gunman materialize out of nowhere. There would have been chaos, panic.

In other words, a normal day for me.

I pulled the bioreader from my pocket. It had been silent since its alert beep at the house, but I had to be sure no one was nearby. Residual effects of the rainstorm made the scan slow, but I waited for the all-clear beep. Closing my eyes against the unpleasant riot of colors that always accompanied porting, I pressed the hidden button on my left cuff and winced at the sudden lurch in my stomach.

When I opened my eyes and saw the look on my partner's face, my stomach churned even worse.

"What the hell was that?" Jara stomped around the end of the console and planted her four-foot, three-inch frame in front of me. The Lathian's magenta eyes glared up into mine.

"It was raining. He got outside before I could apprehend him. The bioreader couldn't pick him up with the rain interfering."

"Bah. You should have snuffed the woman to begin with. She warned him somehow."

I sighed and stepped around her, removing my jacket and holster as I went.

"She's human, Jara. He likes them that way. They amuse him. She couldn't have alerted him without my knowing."

"You'd be surprised what humans can do," she snapped, gliding back to her seat behind the console. "You've been away from them too long."

Another sigh escaped my chest, though I knew it annoyed her and lengthened our arguments. Sometimes I longed for the old days, before I knew anything about Star Services and the...business they conducted.

"Don't play martyr with me again," Jara said, not looking up from her monitors. "You haven't been fully human in quite some time, and that choice was yours."

The truth of her words stung me to silence. I sank into the seat on her right and stared at the viewscreen.

"Your wife called while you were back there," she said after a minute. Her voice had softened a bit.

"Message?"

"Call her before you go back out. And you'd better do it soon, because I just picked him up again."

* * *

I met Jara when I was still human, before I got into this ridiculous mess. I was a computer technician. I had a cheap car, a cracker-box house, and a wife who still loved me.

So, of course, I was bored out of my mind. Easy prey to a group of hunters baiting their trap with adventure and excitement.

I got mugged one night, caught the mugger, and beat him with my briefcase until he stopped moving. That's how they found me - Jara's people, I mean. One moment I was standing over his lifeless body, and the next there was a blinding explosion of colors in front of my eyes. When my vision cleared, Jara was there. She thanked me for catching their "target" for them and offered me a job.

I tried to turn them down, but Jara persuaded me that it was the best thing for my wife and me. She told us about the time travel and how she knew my wife was supposed to die. Whatever else I may have become, I have always loved my wife. She is my greatest strength and my biggest weakness. I agreed to Jara's proposal, even when she told me that the human body could not withstand repeated time travel and I would have to allow them to insert Lathian genes. Then I convinced my wife to move with me to the command center, though I didn't know where that was.

We should both have stayed where we were.

* * *

I stepped into the hall and headed for the televiewer to my right. Trying to keep the strain out of my expression, I dialed home and waited for her answer.

After a few moments, the screen brightened and resolved, revealing a tired pair of blue eyes surrounded by blond hair. My gaze was drawn to the packing boxes behind her.

"Hi babe," I began.

"Look, this is going to be difficult," she interrupted. "Just don't say anything until I'm done, okay?"

It sounds trite, but my heart truly did miss a beat. I knew what was coming, and though I couldn't blame her, I hated it just the same.

"You promised me when you took this job that it was the best thing for both of us. That I was supposed to die some terrible death if I stayed in our time. That your new friends told you so." Her voice cracked on the word "friends", and I wanted to cry with her. But tears were not a part of the "new" me. I was part Lathian now. And Lathians never cry.

"You're not *you* anymore," she said, as though reading my mind. There was no accusation in her tone, but I knew the suspicions had been nibbling at her for some time. "I don't know you. How can I? You're never home; you're always on some weird adventure or another. You promised you'd be home today, as soon as you caught this sicko. You didn't get him, did you?" She hardly waited for my response before continuing.

"That's what I thought. You're going back again. What if you get stuck one of these times? What happens to me then?"

That one hurt. I'd promised to protect her when we came here; humans were all but extinct in this world, and my employers' race was fascinated with them. To the point of experimentation. A human woman left alone among these creatures...

"My point exactly," she said, noticing my shudder. "I want to go home. Even if it means death. I can't take the uncertainty anymore."

"You know what it means to go home?" I didn't need to ask; I'd explained everything to her before we'd agreed to this ridiculous life.

"Yeah, and I know how dangerous the memory wipe is. I'm willing to take the risk." She blotted at her face with her shirtsleeve and flashed me a weak smile. "I love you, baby. I know you can't come with me, not anymore. Whether I remember you or not, some part of me will always miss you."

I nodded, unable to speak.

Jara cleared her throat from the open doorway of the porting center.

"Shel, I have to—"

"—go," she finished for me, and for the first time an edge entered her voice. "Make the arrangements for me before you leave, would you?"

I nodded, but the screen was already dark.

* * *

"He's in 1853," Jara said, punching buttons on the console. "You've got the full five-minute window. Map's on your viewscreen. Make it quick. We can't screw up this time."

We always used Earth time to locate our targets, because I was from that planet and needed an easy frame of reference. The sensors picked up the energy signature of a time-porting Lathian and, if conditions were right, pinpointed him or her to a five-minute frame of time.

Clothes appeared in the window next to the porting dock. Worn, dusty pants and shirt. A brown hat that was sweat-stained and looked as though it had been crushed and re-shaped several times. Two scarred and notched pistol grips peeked out from under a battered gun belt.

Old West Earth. Great. I should fit in there about as well as a hungry tomcat in a mousehole.

* * *

I arrived in an empty field. Knee-high grass swayed in a soft breeze that carried the scent of wildflowers. I had never ported this far back in time, and the silence pressed on my ears.

The bioreader beeped twice, then fell silent. I pulled it from my pocket and turned a full circle. Nothing. Odd. The reader was tuned to the Lathian's unique signature. There was no interference. He should have stood out like a tiger in a field of rabbits.

I sighed and put the reader away. So much for alien tech-nology.

The map had shown a small town nestled behind a hill to the west. Humans were to my target as heroin is to a life-time junkie. I headed toward town, adjusting the odd weight of the gun belt around my hips.

* * *

"Ain't from around here, are ya?" The man who called himself "Bill" narrowed his eyes as he looked me up and down.

"No," I said, trying to look casual as I leaned on the bar. Facing the door, I surveyed the crowd for the hundredth time. "Just lookin' for a friend." My affected accent did not sound natural, and the man frowned.

"Friends're hard to come by in these parts."

I nodded and pulled a folded piece of paper from my pocket. "My friend is easy to spot. He looks like this," I said, losing the fake accent.

As he unfolded the paper, I tensed and settled my hand on my pistol grip, wishing for the sleek handgun I carried in other times. Things were about to get interesting if Bill recognized the figure on that page.

His face paled when he saw the drawing. Bingo.

"Come outside," I said, keeping my voice low. "I want to ask you—"

"Thief!" Shrieking the word as though he'd been struck with a branding iron, he balled up the drawing and threw it aside. Finger pointed in my face, he yelled again, "Stinkin' thief!"

Not the reaction I was expecting, but not too surprising. Instead of killing me himself, he was trying to get the others to do it. "What are you talking about?"

He ignored me and backed away. Glancing at the other patrons, who watched us in varying degrees of surprise, he gestured toward me again. "He's a thief! Hang 'im!"

"What'd he steal?" The bartender's sandpaper voice silenced a murmur that had begun traveling the room. "I didn't see 'im touch nothin'."

I nodded at him in thanks. "I think you're mistaken," I said, watching Bill. "Let's go outside and talk about this."

"Got nothin' to say!" He glared around the room, then spat at my feet. "I'd as soon shoot ya as look at ya. Rotten thief!"

With a sigh, I shoved away from the bar and waved toward the door. "If that's the way you want it. But outside, so we don't mess up this fine gentleman's floor."

By now every pair of eyes in the room was centered on me. My accent and demeanor marked me an outsider—worse, an interesting one. I cursed myself silently. I didn't want an audience. Praying the others wouldn't follow, I nodded toward the door.

After a moment's hesitation, Bill stomped outside, no doubt not wanting to look weak in front of the others. I made my way between the tables, trying to look forbidding. The moment I stepped through the door, I grabbed my would-be accuser and propelled him around the side of the building.

He reached for his pistol, and I pulled mine first. Ramming the barrel into his gut, hard enough to show him I wasn't playing around, I grabbed his gun, threw it aside, and pinned him against the wall.

"Now," I began, shifting my left forearm under his chin so he had to meet my eyes. "Where did you see him?"

"Bastard tol' me another like 'im was comin'. Stole a whole month's pay. I ain't tellin' you nothin' else. You're both a coupla thieves."

I leaned harder on my left arm, cutting off his air supply just a little. He opened his mouth, trying to pull in a full breath. I let him sweat for a minute, then eased up.

"I don't want to hurt you. But my kind don't have the same problems with killing as you people do," I said.

"At least *my* kind stays dead when you kill 'em." He closed his eyes as he mumbled the words.

Imagining the scene that must have played out, I was amused in spite of myself. "You tried to shoot him?"

"I *did* shoot 'im!" He opened his eyes to glare at me. "Hit 'im right through the heart. Tried to get my money back, and the bastard came to life and grabbed my arm." I felt him shudder.

"You didn't hit his heart," I said, not explaining where a Lathian's heart is located.

"Where is he now?"

"Stole a horse an' headed west."

"How long ago?"

He narrowed his eyes and studied me for a moment before answering. "Ain't really his friend, are ya?"

"I don't have any friends," I replied.

Seeming satisfied, Bill said, "Wasn't long ago. Maybe a half hour. I was just gettin' a drink to calm my nerves before tellin' the sheriff."

I released him and glanced at my watch. A half hour was just about the right time frame. "Thanks. Why the change of heart?"

Grinning, he spat at my feet again. "Maybe you two can kill each other."

"Yes. Thank you." *At least he's honest,* I thought as I turned away.

"If ya catch him, bring my money back, would ya?"

* * *

Ten minutes outside of town, I decided I hated horses. All creatures with hooved feet and small brains, in fact.

I hadn't ridden a horse since high school, and this one did not seem happy about being stolen from his peaceful nap behind the saloon. Ears laid back, he flatly refused to move faster than a sort of bouncing run-walk that made both my head and my seat sore.

Just as I was contemplating the possible outcomes of shooting the horse between the ears, we topped a ridge and found a narrow depression, the center of which was occupied by a black horse tied to a dying tree. My mount, apparently deciding that there was safety in numbers, leaped into a headlong gallop that left me sprawling on my back in the dirt.

Decision made. I was going to shoot him.

Wincing at the stabbing pain in my back, I picked myself up and took a good look around, wondering where the new horse's rider had gone. A small creek gurgled past the tree and disappeared around a bend. This little valley appeared deserted.

As I approached the horses, my mount abandoned his comrade and ran, tail and head held high, several hundred yards downstream. I ignored him, bidding him good riddance.

The black snorted as I placed a hand on his neck, but went back to grazing when I made no attempt to mount. Finely-tooled saddlebags hung across the animal's rump, and I opened the nearest one. It contained nothing but a folded piece of paper on which was written two words: Try Again.

I cursed, recognizing the handwriting, and reached for the button on my cuff.

* * *

"He threw me off," Jara said by way of greeting. "He's been baiting us."

"Then what's he really up to?" I asked, irritation and fatigue wearing on my nerves. Pulling clothes out of the window next to the porting dock, I was relieved to see a T-shirt and jeans. My relief faded when I turned around and caught the pity in Jara's eyes.

"He's gone back to your time. He arrived there a few minutes after your wife did."

* * *

Even with Lathian genes, porting is hard on the human body. One or two never bothered me, but several trips in a short span of time, plus a bouncy ride on a stubborn horse, made my entire body feel as though I'd been danced on by said horse. My joints ached, my head buzzed like it contained a thousand angry wasps, and my eyes felt grainy.

Worse, I was nearly crippled with worry over my wife. In all the chaos that was my life, I had allowed myself to forget how much I loved her. It all came crashing back to me now, until I thought I would be crushed under the weight of emotion.

I ported into the living room of the small house we'd shared. Jara didn't want to send me there; she was worried that our target was there and the clashing energy signatures would cause an accident.

I insisted.

As the living room resolved around me, I was struck with another emotion: nostalgia. I realized for the first time how much I missed this place and the "boring" life I'd led here.

A woman's voice, singing an old song, reminded me why I was here. I tensed, hoping she would not enter the living room and panic at the sight of me. I would be a stranger to her now; the memory wipe was very thorough. After a moment, I realized I could hear water running, and relaxed.

Shel always liked to sing in the shower.

Beginning to worry about the time I was wasting on sentimentality, I pulled the bioreader from my pocket. It had turned itself to silent mode, which meant my target was very close. My heart dropped into my shoes when the reader's screen went red. He was within a few feet.

He had to be inside the apartment.

Shel was still singing, and I wished she would shut up. She was leading him right to her.

Keeping low, I stepped around the threadbare couch and paused next to the door leading to the hallway. I strained to hear something other than my wife's voice, but she was doing a wonderful job of masking all other sounds.

I took a deep breath to calm my racing heart and burst into the hallway, sweeping my gun in an arc to cover the far end.

The hallway was deserted.

The singing stopped.

My wife screamed. The pain and terror in her voice spurred me down the hall, into the master bedroom, and toward the bathroom door. Steam curled out through the cracks, along with the scent of lavender soap.

Before I was halfway across the bedroom, the screaming stopped.

A horrible, blinding rage like I have never experienced before or since swept through me then. These creatures had stolen my life, my personality, and now my wife. I had no family but her.

And now she was gone.

I tore the bathroom door open and charged inside. The Lathian I'd been hunting crouched over my wife's unmoving body. Her face was turned toward me, and the accusation I imagined in her eyes was worse than a kick in the stomach. Blood pooled around her shoulders.

The Lathian stood up and turned his red eyes on me. His snout was flecked with blood. He leered at me.

"Halfer," he said, using the derogatory term Lathians used for altered humans like me. "You're late. You've missed all the fun."

"Fun's just starting," I replied before emptying my gun's magazine into him. When I ran out of ammunition, I began beating him with my fists.

I was still pummeling his corpse when Jara arrived to retrieve me.

* * *

I was supposed to bring him in alive. That was my job. Punishment for failure is swift and severe.

So I write this narrative from the chair I'm bound to. The Lathians broke both my legs. To Jara's credit, she tried to intervene on my behalf. Good thing the punishment for failure is not as severe for a Lathian as for a halfer.

My chair sits in a sunny room painted in pastels that are supposed to be soothing. White-jacketed people move among us, the living dead, handing out medication and reassuring words.

Their words are empty. Nothing reassures me now.

They say I'm crazy. They found me pinned under a truck outside my apartment building. They don't believe me when I tell them the Lathians planted me there.

Why should they believe? It's a ridiculous story about a ridiculous life.

My doctor is a man named Shelton Ryan Alexander. He laughs when I tell him his name is backwards. He thinks I am witty, but he also thinks I'm a kook. He would never tell me that he thinks I'm a kook, but I know it. It's written in his eyes and the condescending way he smiles at my stories. He, and all the nurses, call me "Tom". It is nice, not being called "Halfer."

I tried to tell them, when I first came here, all about the Lathians and what they do. About how my wife wound up dead.

They told me, gently, that my mind was creating a cover to hide the awful truth from myself that I'd killed my wife. It's nonsense, of course, but I can't blame them. I'd have thought the same thing, once upon a time.

Now I sit here, day after day. I am cooperative and charming, a favorite among the nurses. They don't know my real secret. They don't know I'm just biding my time.

For the Lathians, in all their careful planning, managed to overlook one thing.

I still have a remote button for the porting dock. It was on my cuff when they placed me in front of that truck. I have managed to keep it hidden all this time. I've realized that the only way to make up for the work I did for the Lathians is to stop their operation. It's the only way to honor the memory of Shel, my poor trusting wife.

Someday, Dr. Alexander will pronounce me healthy and release me from this hospital.

By then, I will have a plan.

I will pay the Lathians one last visit.

Then I'll show them how well they trained their "halfer" hit-man.

Courting
ChaosInOrder

Spinning slowly, you are graceful in the soft yellow light
My hand, still pointed
palm up
Stretched at the end of my arm
A single strand of emotion connects us
Invisible
Only the two of us know
We are inseparable

Your eyes are closed
Un-needed
The strand connects
You see through me
As you escape
Momentarily free
Of everything
But me

No sound exists beyond our minds
The rhythm driving your silky revolutions
Needs no stirrup or conch
It need not come in to your brain from outside
The notes have never played
The melody was never written
The sound of two souls
forever connected
One hand clapping
A tree in the forest
With no one to hear
The vibrations of love
Need no-one to hear
Only two to feel

The twirls of forever
Now slow
And stop on this physical plane
Our eyes
Perfectly locked
Across the geometric expanse
The smiles are there
Though nobody knows
They look to the lips and miss the eyes
If they knew they wouldn't believe
Their big brains
So full of useless knowledge
Could not conceive
Something so perfectly empty
And wonderfully full

My left arm rises to meet the right
The strand now double necked
Jimmy Paige pounding twelve strings as one
Becomes 2
It is not strengthened
Nor diluted
The riff of our devotion
Just as it has always been
And shall always be
The invisible bond
Between I
And thee

Fingers curl slowly
A fist that isn't cocked
A clench that seeks not to hold
But release, and protect
Draws you back to my embrace
You tumble, forward and free
Five revolutions bring you to me
Now cheek to cheek
My hand on your hip
Back where we started
This eternal trip
Though never ending
begins once again

à votre santé

Oblivion
Stephen W. Cote

NOTHING LIKE HEAVEN

They were new. It showed. The youthful men strode in merriment, following an athletic trail that meandered through a park, skirting the edge of the Myrrh Desert. Newcomers were attracted to the desert by the magnificent color of the silty, reddish-gray sand. It was the only natural feature radiating color for as far as one could see. The single faint color was amplified by the molten blackness of the adjacent Obsidian Sea. The landscape cast its own eerie luminescence and no light shone from the pitch-black and starless sky. At the edge of the Myrrh Desert, the reality of all newcomers' situation settled in when they checked their tour map and correctly identified their location. More specifically, the newcomers discovered why the sand had color. The sand was gray and the color bled from afterworld two hundred ninety nine, Human Christian Hell.

The effect had more meaning to Human Christians than anyone else. No matter the response, the newcomers were bound to notice another unnerving sight: the firm grip of senility engrossing the abandoned stares of most people lounging in the park. In the moment when a newcomer first witnesses those near-lifeless souls, particularly one of their own species, the germ of their destiny begins to fester. Ultimately, the newcomers realize they are looking upon themselves many years hence, when they have resigned to live an eternal afterlife without conscious thought and mental faculty.

"Droolers," a passerby explained to the slack-jawed and awestruck newcomers. "After you've been stuck in a Ghost Box, captured in a spirit battery, visited a few of the afterworlds where you only see the world in black-and-white and can never stay, tried to kill yourself, overfed every vice you crave and in sheer boredom sought those vices you always thought were beyond your interest, you'll find your way here." The passerby nodded knowingly and looked upon a Drooler with a resigned and emotionally stunted expression. "One day you will give up completely. You will realize there is no where else to go and nothing else to do, and then you will plant yourself on one of these benches and start to drool."

A newcomer waved his hand in front of a Drooler's eyes. She appeared youthful and had a vibrant and healthy tone to her body, but she was hunched forward and her watery eyes sought a nonexistent point on the horizon. "I'll never let myself be in such a sorry state!" the newcomer declared.

The air was filled with cynical laughter and the passerby left the newcomers to contemplate their next move.

A spastic twitch channeled through a tiny wrinkle of skin just below Tif Brown's left eyelid. It was her first movement in over three months. The word Drooler entered her mind as a dreamy and sluggish abstraction of what she knew the word to describe. But she couldn't bring herself to care, or remember what had captivated her attention. Her mouth was wet with spittle and her incessant, never-ending drool soaked the front of her shirt. Unfiltered nihilism was ground into her entire spirit and there came no further active thought or movement.

Tif had never known of a Drooler to return to active consciousness. She had not left the bench for more than five Earth years. Her eyes were unfocused on the utter grayness of this afterworld, blurring it into a bright sepia tone. She could not remember when she last saw that color, and was unable to contemplate the hazy faux-color tone being so far from self-recognition. It couldn't be a color. Not here. Spittle blotted the corners of her mouth. She had no motivation to exist, held in the infinite grip of Oblivion.

BRANGOT AND DIOTITUS

Brangot heaved a heavy fist of tightly knotted roots against his neighbor's apartment door. When no answer came, he rapped the door with two fists, his other two fists holding a towel around his naked trunk. Soapy water dripped from his bark and leafy skin onto Diotitus' doormat. He knew there would be no response at Tif's door. She was a Drooler in Myrrh Desert Park and hadn't been home in several years.

Diotitus opened the door and gave a wry grin upon seeing the wet and mostly naked warrior. The hulking plant warrior appeared flustered and Diotitus offered, "Greek bath? It's been a few millennia, but I'm sure I can recall those techniques that really curled your leaves."

"We have to talk," Brangot declared and pushed his way into Diotitus' tiny apartment. He had to stoop so as not to bump his head-branches on the doorframe.

"Hold on," Diotitus rushed past Brangot. "I just polished my ceremonial armor and you'll get it wet. That hard water you like to bath in will leave mineral deposits."

Brangot shot one of his long arms around Diotitus and forcefully shut the door. "We've got a problem. We need to get Tif. Now."

As Brangot had expected, Diotitus was completely unphased. "She's gone," he said soberly. "Been gone for a while," he twirled his finger at the side of his head to indicate insanity. "The managers know she's at the park and are ready to reassign her room."

Brangot shook his head, sending water droplets flying around the room. "I realize her situation. But, now we have our own situation related to hers."

"What?" Diotitus exclaimed irritably, trying to herd the much larger plant warrior towards the door. "Why don't you dry off and then tell me what's got your leaves all wrinkled?"

"When a god sends you a message in the shower, you don't stop to dry off." Brangot explained in an exasperated tone, not letting Diotitus crowd him out of the room.

Diotitus sized over Brangot, trying to ascertain the context of what now sounded like one of his extremely dry jokes. "And?" he asked, unconvinced.

"You and I have been summoned to the Conservatory," Brangot said, and waited for Diotitus to grasp the implication.

"You had better not be joking," Diotitus said firmly. "Why would the two of us be invited there? Well," he nodded in sublime arrogance, "I could see why I might be invited."

"No," Brangot snapped, "It has nothing to do with your five minutes as a *Grick* god with, how many worshippers did you say there were? Four?"

"*Greek* god, and it was ten," Diotitus snapped. "And it was for four months. At least three, anyway." He picked up a half-polished circlet lying on a stack of clay-tablet magazines. "If we were not asked to the Conservatory because of my long-standing status as a god," and Diotitus leveled his index finger at Brangot, "and because I was grandfathered in before the billion-worshipper rule was enacted doesn't change the fact. Anyway, if not because of my status, then why would we be invited?"

"Tif," Brangot said simply. "Something to do with Tif is all I was told. And whatever it is, we'll eventually have to get her."

Diotitus exhaled a lengthy sigh, turned the circlet in his fingers, and tossed it back to its place of prominence on top of the clay tablets. "They're gods," he said matter-of-factly. "They must know we can't simply shake her a bit and wake her up."

Brangot adjusted his towel and shrugged anxiously. "I told them she was a Drooler. I figured they would know what I meant."

"What could they possibly want with a Drooler?" Diotitus mused. "And how would we get her back? She may be physically a couple of blocks away, but she's long gone."

Brangot shrugged. "I didn't ask. When you get a message from multiple gods of significant stature, you don't waste time asking."

"More than one god? And you didn't take the time to ask who they were or what exactly we were supposed to do with a Drooler?" Diotitus asked incredulously.

"No," Brangot said, annoyed. "Like I said, I told them she was a Drooler, but they didn't appear to understand. Maybe they were gods with a GeD. I didn't get the impression they spent much time around here."

"Great," Diotitus said and became deflated. "So you want to come running because a bunch of bookworms with their God-like effect Doctorates called? They're the only ones at the Conservatory anyway because they don't have another afterworld of their own."

"I don't know who it was," Brangot droned. "But when was the last time a god called you to the Conservatory?"

Diotitus didn't answer. In the seemingly eternal amount of time he had spent in this afterworld, no god had ever summoned him. "So what did Tif do? Maybe some god she had a fling with?"

"Don't get sour because she never had any interest in you," Brangot said. He wadded the towel in his leafy knuckles and looked expectantly at Diotitus. "Well, are you coming?"

"What, now?" Diotitus asked.

"Yes, now. Right now. Get in your in-a-god's-presence best and let's go."

Diotitus motioned at Brangot. "You're not going like that, are you?"

"I don't take half as long as you do to get dressed," Brangot replied.

SPIRIT CHANNEL

Diotitus, clad in his brass and linen appointments, and Brangot, wearing a heavily woven bark uniform, trotted down the Channel Access Road towards the recently constructed

Spirit Channel Station. Diotitus carried a small iron shield and a royal baton. Brangot's upper arms were devoted to carrying a long cylindrical weapon used primarily for ceremonial display, while his two lower arms swung at his side. As they neared the station, they could see a crowd of people meandering aimlessly in the street.

Diotitus came to a halt and cursed. "New arrivals mobbing the station. What, they think they can get into some heaven?"

Brangot prodded Diotitus forward. "New souls now arrive from the channel instead of bulk freight delivery. Change of policy from a few months ago."

"They need to get organized," Diotitus snapped.

The two wove through the dazed crowd, ignoring the plethora of routine questions asked by new arrivals. They found themselves boxed in by a party of space explorers as they approached the channel and the crowd thickened.

One of the explorers raised a probe towards Brangot, and said, "We are explorers from the planet …"

Brangot gently pushed through the explorers without remark.

Diotitus was less kind. He stopped by the explorer with the probe and chided, "You're dead and you're stuck here for eternity. Go to the relocation center to get your flat assignment." Without waiting for a response, he pushed through the explorers and followed Brangot.

Diotitus and Brangot walked through the entrance of the Spirit Channel Station, which was an open-air platform beside an ethereal river. The boarding line was short and the agent processed travelers at a brisk pace.

"Destination," the agent asked.

"Conservatory," Brangot answered.

The agent held up a scanner and waved it across Diotitus' chest, and then Brangot's trunk. "Are either of you carrying any spirit batteries?"

Both shook their heads.

The agent nodded and said, "So you're aware, we're checking those now." The agent stowed the scanner and then rapid-fired a series of questions. "Are either of you agents of the Trans-Dimensional Nexus? Are either of you carrying artifacts or souvenirs from In-Life or Pre-Life brought to this world by someone other than yourselves? Have you ever been damned for a period equal to or longer than an eternity, and if so, when did you qualify for release?"

Both answered no.

"Have you arranged for accommodations at the Conservatory?"

Again, they shook their heads.

"The entirety of the Universe, including all known and unknown dimensions, is currently in a paradox recovery cycle. The Spirit Channel will travel out of Oblivion and through afterworld one to reach afterworld sixteen, the Conservatory, and you will be arriving fourteen hours in the past." The agent handed them their boarding passes. "Since you will be traveling to a non-observation level of an afterworld, you will experience strong perceptions of color." The agent pointed towards his eyes. "You may need to give yourself a few minutes to adjust when you arrive. Have a nice ride."

Brangot and Diotitus walked briskly towards a car marked clearly for the Generally Unsaved, and boarded. They found two uncomfortable and cramped seats near the back and stowed their ceremonial appointments in an overhead storage vat.

Once seated, Brangot hunched forward so his head

branches weren't touching the overhead vat. "I hope this is a short ride," he muttered.

"Okay, we're arriving fourteen hours ago?" Diotitus asked. "It took me long enough to wrap my head around time not being linear, and segment repetition to resolve disputes. But this is the first I've heard of this paradox recovery nonsense."

Brangot nodded then shrugged. "I gather when some idiot fusses with time and wipes out a part of the In-Life universe, they go into recovery mode. Or, maybe they're replaying past events until time starts moving forward again. You do know In-Life time has not advanced in a number of years, right?" Brangot looked out the window and down into the ethereal river, momentarily wondering why a train would travel on a river. He mused, "I've forgotten when time was not in some sort of cycle and was moving forward." He tried to look ahead in the direction the Spirit Channel would take them, saying, "It will be nice to see real color again."

Diotitus sat back in his seat. "I'm in color," he declared and looked down at the glossy orange and gold tones of his ceremonial dress. "And you're in color," he pointed at Brangot's woven garment. "A muted flat green, I think."

"But nothing else is in color," Brangot said. "You know what I mean."

Diotitus rapped Brangot's lower left shoulder, producing a muted knocking sound, and laughed. "I think you're guessing about the recovery cycle." He then shrugged. "I can never keep track of what is happening in the In-Life Universe. They keep replaying parts of it, or in this case, recycling it. They call it a paradox, but you know it's all about the gods acquiring as many worshippers as possible."

Brangot shifted in his seat in a futile attempt to maintain

a passable comfort level, then looked at Diotitus and raised a leafy eyebrow. "Tell me again why you're in the unsaved car and not traveling god-class?"

Diotitus muttered under his breath and held his knees against the back of the seat in front of him so his feet dangled above the ground. "I suppose if we're arriving in the past this won't take too long."

Brangot laughed, "Not as long as the first time, I hope."

Diotitus looked at him quizzically. "And how long was that? Did this contraption break down?"

"The channel wasn't calibrated for traveling between time zones the first time it crossed between two afterworlds, and it didn't show up for a couple years." Brangot pushed a few leafy fingers at the window. "The station went unused for several years while the channel was lost in time. If you bothered to walk two blocks from our building you would have noticed."

Diotitus shrugged. "I suppose whoever wants to meet with us will make sure that sort of thing doesn't happen. But," he added thoughtfully, "If this is so important, they could have sprung for better seats."

Some minutes later, Diotitus mused aloud, "So, is it a train or a channel?" though Brangot offered no response.

Both men remained quiet and rode in silence as the Spirit Channel whisked them along the ethereal river. Periodically, the Channel swept out of Oblivion for a fraction of a second, and bands of bright star- and sky-wept colors flashed against the window. The Channel never left Oblivion or the empty, muted plains of afterworld one for more than a brief moment, though passengers were able to board and depart at the appropriate destination.

Brangot reached across Diotitus with one arm when the

colorful bands struck the window and pressed his leafy fingers flat against the glass. He breathed in slowly, filling his mouth and throat with what he thought of as the air touched by the real and after worlds.

"Look," He whispered into Diotitus' ear and Diotitus stirred in his light slumber. "Color," Brangot said, and Diotitus opened his eyes.

Diotitus imagined he could feel a playful caress of color splashing against his face. "How long has it been?" he asked, not looking away from the window.

"I don't remember," Brangot said in a tone encompassing awe and remorse. "I think I dreamed of my native indigo sky a few decades ago."

Diotitus was on the cusp of asking Brangot more about his home world, a topic Brangot was particularly mysterious about. However, the Sprit Channel appeared to slow down, the world went white, and they were alone.

THE CONSERVATORY

The entrance to the Conservatory was abstract. It wasn't as much of a place as it was an architectural expression of its members. The entrance appeared to be a concave forum of silk and padding, surrounded by a mild convex plateau of flower petals. As Diotitus and Brangot recovered their sight, they found themselves immersed in bright palettes of pastels, deep reds, and light pinks. Though fully toned and brilliant, the light was nevertheless softly cast so as to produce no shadow.

Both men stood in awe of the color.

"How do I look?" Diotitus whispered. The din of their afterworld was gone, and he found his whisper boomed in the sterling silence.

Brangot quickly checked his clothes and appointments, and then surveyed Diotitus. "Fix your circlet."

Diotitus groped the top of his head and adjusted the circlet to rest evenly on his crown.

"Where do you think we are supposed to go?" Brangot asked.

Then, a tower appeared as though Brangot's words compelled it into existence. The tower was of such stature and opulence that Brangot swooned, and was overcome with extreme vertigo. Its smooth form was pearl-toned and its presence lashed up at a brilliant sky that moments before appeared to be little more than an abstract ceiling with a soft and silky décor.

Diotitus looked up at Brangot, then back at the tower. "I see a door, I think." He started walking towards the tower, and Brangot followed at his side.

The tower appeared larger as the men walked towards it, but they couldn't determine how close they were. It kept growing bigger.

After walking for ten minutes, a voice spoke from behind them.

"An illusion," the voice said, and both men spun round, coming face to face with someone they took for a god.

Brangot's heart raced and he raised his cylindrical weapon in salute.

Diotitus was slow to follow, but he caught himself gawking and he offered an affable salute with his shield and baton.

"Brangot, Diotitus," the apparent god said. His presence was spectacular in its grace and form, and his voice was a sonorous experience closer to a symphony than mere words. "My name is Brian." Brian looked at both of the men for a moment, and then commented, "Was it made clear you were to bring Tif?"

Diotitus raised an eyebrow and looked at Brangot.

"The subject was broached," Brangot said, pausing to find an appropriate salutation. "Sir," he concluded.

"Tif isn't available," Diotitus responded with a measure of caution in his voice. "I was told that information had been passed on to you."

Brian's lips turned into a mild frown, and the once bright disposition of his voice changed to suit, becoming more intimidating. "Should I conclude your presence is to trifle with my patience?"

"Uh, no," Diotitus started.

"Then where is Tif?" Brian demanded. Clouds billowed up in the sky and were tortured by a bolt of lightning. Cracking thunder rang in their ears.

"Sir," Brangot said, and though mindful of the god's show of pageantry felt otherwise unmoved, "She is not sound of mind, and is completely unresponsive to any outside stimuli. Perhaps you might have better luck if you went to her?"

Brian snarled his lip, though his expression relaxed. "We don't go there," he sneered.

Diotitus thought Brian's tone sounded somewhat snide, and he looked more closely at the god-like form. He stood as tall as Diotitus, who was much shorter than Brangot. His shoulders were hunched forward a bit, and as Diotitus forced himself to look less at his god-like presence and more at him as a person, he noticed Brian was fidgeting with his hands.

Brangot raised his lower set of arms in appeasement, "Sir, perhaps if I explained …" but Brian cut him off.

"I want results, not explanations," Brian fumed.

Diotitus grew less impressed and more impatient. Real Gods, the honest-to-goodness birthed-from-the-fires-of-the-universe Gods, didn't hang around the Conservatory. He knew that much. These were academic gods. Bookworm gods.

Diotitus glanced sidelong at Brangot and a wry grin crossed his face. "I've got three spirit batteries that say he's only a junior, with at least four thousand years to go."

Brangot was ready to snap at Diotitus when Brangot felt that his friend's words rang true. Brian carried himself with an amateurish disposition, and demeaned himself as a bore. Brangot held up the business end of his cylindrical weapon, pointing it towards Brian. "Care to settle our little bet? Do you have your degree?"

Brian raised his hand as though he was ready to work some miracle, and Brangot smartly rapped his knuckles with the end of the long cylinder.

"Ow!" Brian whined and sucked the back of his hand. "I never said I was a god. You assumed."

Diotitus pushed his way past Brian, and Brangot went out of his way to push his way past him as well, and the two men continued walking towards the tower.

"What do you suppose that was about?" Brangot asked when he thought Brian was out of earshot.

"He knew who Tif was," Diotitus said. "I would say it was for some lofty reason, but I'm partial to thinking one of the gods sent him to meet us if for no other reason than to be an ass."

"Why would you think that?" Brangot asked.

"Because we're from the sewer of the universe," Diotitus said. "And these guys spent fifteen thousand years or more getting the most prestigious degree possible. They're academics, and they have degrees to be gods. What good is that if you can't lord it over everyone else?"

Brangot nodded, considering Diotitus' jaded view. "I find it curious they didn't go see Tif themselves. Do you think it's a stigma against being in our afterworld?"

"Arrogance?" Diotitus offered. "Or maybe they can't get in to our afterworld?" he said in jest.

"Maybe they can't," Brangot said soberly. "I never really thought about it, but perhaps there are places in the afterlife where gods cannot go."

After a long though peaceful walk, they arrived at a large door leading into the tower. The door was constructed of black iron and aged wood planks. It was blocked open with a wooden wedge. Standing outside of the tower, they could feel the air inside was cool and dusty, smelling of granite, wood grains, and linseed oil.

Brangot, followed by Diotitus, entered and approached a large, simple wooden desk. A young man greeted them with a broad smile and bid them a good morning.

"You must be Diotitus," he said.

Diotitus nodded and leaned over the desk to read the man's name, which was scrawled on a sticker and applied to his nondescript uniform. "Rick?"

Rick looked up at Brangot. "And you must be Brangot."

Brangot presented Rick with a lesser manual salutation befitting secretaries and concierges. Brangot noticed Diotitus offered no salutation at all.

Rick narrowed his eyes slightly while looking at Brangot. "I hope you don't think me too impulsive, but I can't place your home world."

Brangot didn't respond, so Diotitus replied, "no one knows, and he never talks about it."

"I see," Rick said thoughtfully.

"Rick, not to be dismissive, but we were called here on urgent business," Brangot said, hoping to get off the topic of his home world. "I wouldn't want anyone to be waiting for us."

Rick continued to smile. "Not at all. In fact, they are waiting for you in the conference room on the thirty thousandth floor. You'll want to take the elevator." He motioned towards a pair of black, polished steel doors set into a medieval stone wall on the far side of the lobby.

The men thanked Rick and walked across the lobby to the elevator. The doors opened when they approached, then closed when they entered, and started moving up.

"Weird," Diotitus said. "This place, I've decided, is extraordinarily weird."

"Actually, it's making more sense now that we're inside," Brangot said. "It has all of the artistry of a college. Isn't that what this is? A college for people studying to be gods?"

Diotitus shrugged. "I never had to study."

"I like it," Brangot decided. "It is refreshing to not be surrounded by unnecessary technology and otherworldly machinations. Did you notice Rick was using a quill and homemade paper?"

"It's not a monastery," Diotitus snorted. "I think they're taking it too far."

The trip was short, and the elevator stopped moving and the doors opened to reveal a large, open-air conference room. A sky at twilight illuminated a central desk with a soft glow, and Diotitus thought he could hear crickets chirping and frogs croaking in the distance.

"Gentlemen," a steely voice spoke. A man with thin gray

hair, drawn features, and wizened countenance approached them. "Gerard," he said, pronouncing the first syllable as a silence-baiting consonant.

"Brangot," Brangot said and offered his formal salutation using his lower arms to extend his cylindrical weapon and his upper arms to show he held no other armament.

"Diotitus," Diotitus said and grudgingly offered his own formal greeting, though had started to feel academic gods shouldn't deserve it. He only half bowed and didn't complete the full salutary motion with the baton.

Gerard looked over both men, and a thin smile drew across his pasty lips. "I hope it hurt," he said, glancing along the length of the polished cylindrical weapon held in Brangot's lower hands. "Tell me," he said to Diotitus, "how did you know he didn't have his degree?"

"He showed us some nice parlor tricks, but he didn't strike me as having a god-like presence." Diotitus shrugged.

"Indeed." Gerard said. He remained quiet for a moment and then beckoned them towards the large table. "Let's sit and I will tell you why you were summoned."

The two men set their appointments on the floor and sat down in the large and very comfortable chairs surrounding the table.

"This is a nice effect you have," Diotitus said, nodding towards the ceiling that looked and felt like they were under an open sky. He fully appreciated being bathed in the soft, colorful light and observing the different hues and tones.

"I had thought you might like it. It's a Greek sky from your lifetime." Gerard offered another thin smile.

Diotitus, never much of a reveler of the sky when alive, now took a careful look at his surroundings for it then seemed very similar to the architecture and environment from his homeland.

Gerard sat down at the table next to Brangot, folded his hands, and placed them on the table. "I'm sorry your friend could not be roused, but I am aware her condition makes it difficult." He nodded towards Brangot, "You were correct in thinking we cannot enter Oblivion, which is why we were hoping you would bring Tif here. Although, it doesn't matter where she is since she is a fully repressed." He paused, and momentarily appended, "I believe the popular term right now is Drooler. But she has become of significant import and I hope to task the two of you with the responsibility of waking her."

"I never thought that was possible," Diotitus said.

"She's hasn't completely repressed herself," Gerard advised, and looking directly at Diotitus, continued, "and if you ever gave serious thought to making some positive contribution in her life, then you would at least try to help her."

Diotitus nodded slightly.

"Can you tell us why it is so important that she recover?" Brangot asked.

Gerard nodded. "First, I would like to discuss with you the reasons that brought you to the Conservatory." He paused and looked between Brangot and Diotitus. "The main reason is both of you have known Tif the longest, and self repression is not an abnormality cured with a snap of a god's fingers. It is a psychological ill, and she will need her friends, the two of you, to convince her that her existence is worth experiencing."

"I'm surprised you can't help her," Diotitus said plainly. "I had always assumed gods to be more or less omnipotent."

"Ah," Gerard said with a broader smile, "A misunderstanding. Gods are more or less omnipotent in their afterworlds, and have varying abilities to interact with In-

Life and Pre-Life. Oblivion is a special case. It is not my intention to foster ill will here, but Oblivion isn't an afterworld. It is a nexus between all other known and unknown dimensions. While the gods would eagerly support moving the entire population to an afterworld, no god has any real power or authority over it." He spread out his hands on the table, and concluded his answer by adding, "to be clear, gods not only have little to no power in Oblivion, most can't even enter it. And, the same goes for many afterworlds. A god in one afterworld may carry the title into another afterworld, but certainly not the power."

"Everyone who has studied for a god degree is only a god at the Conservatory?" Diotitus asked.

Gerard nodded. "Yes. However, many afterworlds employ our graduates for research and administrative purposes, and they are permitted to use some or all of their skills in the other afterworlds."

"Except Oblivion," Brangot said thoughtfully. "Because there is no god to grant access."

"Correct," Gerard said. "Another reason why we asked you to come is because it is easier for you to cross between Oblivion and an afterworld than it is for anyone who has been categorized into an afterworld to enter Oblivion. Granted, you would need credentials to get beyond the black-and-white observation levels of a given afterworld, but those are easier to acquire than someone from an afterworld trying to gain access to Oblivion. Also, there is the simple fact that the majority of afterworld inhabitants are not interested in Oblivion. They perceive it as another type of Christian Limbo."

"You want us to wake up Tif, and go on a tour of some afterworlds?" Diotitus asked, perplexed.

"That's not the half of it," Gerard said with a smile

intimating both subtle humor and deep concern. "The moment Tif became a Drooler, she was thinking about something. We want you to finish her thought, and put it into motion."

"What is the value of Tif's last, half-finished thought?" Brangot asked. "Why is it so important?"

"Unfortunately, I can't elaborate why it's important. I can only say she was thinking about a method to track every particle in the known universe over time."

Diotitus caught himself before letting out a guffaw. "Tif was thinking that? Why would such nonsense even matter? Maybe for research, I suppose."

"It's very important," Gerard explained. "Having a brief stint as a god yourself, you should know why it is important. The explanation is quite simple. If you mutilate a body at the time of death, and disperse the parts over a wide area, the soul is also dispersed. What percentage of a soul is required to be claimed as a worshipper by a god?"

Brangot looked at Diotitus, who shrugged. "I have no idea."

"Fifty-one percent," Gerard continued. "A god may claim a soul as a worshipper if they have fifty-one percent of it. Good for the god and the respective afterworld, and good for at least fifty-one percent of the soul. However, the other forty-nine percent will be missing. We surmise most of these soul fragments wind up in spirit batteries or stuck in Ghost Boxes. They don't have the insight to know to avoid those things."

"Now," Gerard went on, "imagine what would happen if an entire world was destroyed."

"How exactly would that happen?" Diotitus asked, but was nudged by Brangot.

"Read the news sometime," Brangot whispered irritably.

"It happens," Gerard said. "And, when it does, it is rare to recover a significant portion of a soul because the soul is scattered across the universe. Trans-dimensional fish food, to use an unsympathetic description."

"Now," he said and leveled his gaze at the two men. "What if something like that happened, which we call a Grand Disaster, and we had been able to track every particle. We could use the data to filter the scattered soul particles from the Quantum Stream and fully reassemble each and every soul because we would have known where a soul was at the time of the disaster, and where all of the particles comprising the soul had been dispersed."

"How exactly would that work?" Diotitus asked, not fully understanding what Gerard was saying.

"Tif knows," Brangot submitted. "Right?"

Gerard nodded. "Precisely. No one has ever worked out how this could be accomplished, except Tif. But, even she didn't figure it all out. There still remains the issue of how to record and access all of the data."

"A lot of information," Diotitus commented.

"You have no idea," Gerard stated.

"Haven't the gods figured this sort of thing out?" Diotitus asked.

"Genetic mathematics?" Brangot offered.

Gerard nodded. "And, here we encounter one of many problems. The Creation Mathematics used to create the basis of life is a closely guarded secret. No one will give it to you. All I can tell you is we need you to complete Tif's thought as much as possible, and help her recover from her repression. I will arrange for you to gain access to any afterworlds you consider necessary to meet these tasks. You already have access to the Quantum Stream."

"Not a very exciting place," Diotitus remarked, and Brangot nodded in agreement.

Gerard smiled. "I imagine you'll be spending a lot of time there."

"What if we are unable or unwilling to do this?" Brangot asked.

"Universal Standard Time hasn't moved forward in a very long time, and we can't let it move forward until this matter is addressed. However, some gods are growing very irritable over the constant recovery cycles as such cycles alter their worshipper base. Of course, I can't force either of you to do anything. But, don't you at least want to help your friend?"

"Suppose we do attempt this impossible feat," Diotitus asked. "What then?"

Gerard looked at them plainly. "In all honesty, I can't promise there would be a reward." Then, he chuckled. "You want a mountain of gold bullion, or a fancy chariot?"

"Possessions are useless to us," Brangot commented.

"Which makes a reward unrealistic," Gerard said.

Diotitus sat back in his chair and thought about the request. He felt like Gerard was looking for a couple unsaved lackeys, and was trying to steal the thoughts of a mostly-insane woman. Images of Tif crossed his mind and he felt utterly helpless about waking her from her drooling state. Seated beneath a sky deemed to be his own, his mere moments of In-Life fluttered across the recesses of his mind. He recalled his childhood of privilege, youthful adventures as a Greek soldier, his promotion to commander, and his brief and limited ascension to the status of a god. In the handful of weeks when his god-like-effect powers were supposed to be at their height, he couldn't even muster a rain cloud or enchant a rune. It was all a sham.

Now, seated alongside an academically certified god, his claims to be a god were laughable. At least Gerard and his peers had studied for many millennia. What deeds qualified him to be a god, and what did he have to show for his reign? A few clay tablets advertising his ascension. His fall was heralded only by the migration of his few worshippers. No one had been left with any concern to finish the epic of Diotitus.

Diotitus momentarily forgot why Brangot and he were necessary at all. *Because the gods don't have any power in Oblivion.* His spiral into depression took an immediate turn in the opposite direction as he thought less about what he was able to do, and more about what Gerard and the other gods couldn't do. They couldn't use their powers in Oblivion, and in many cases, they couldn't even enter it. Oblivion may have been the sewer and the plumbing of the afterworlds, but it was also the afterworld of the forgotten. *There were no gods of Oblivion.*

Diotitus touched Brangot's arm to get his attention, and then offered him a slight nod and a subtle smile. He looked at Gerard and said, "I think we may be able to work something out."

Brangot raised a bark-crusted brow though said nothing.

"I presume if we complete this task, which sounds like it would be a service, it would have to be administered and maintained," Diotitus mused.

"Yes," Gerard nodded, though his features betrayed reservation. "The Time Stream is managed by some machine-people and I imagine they would like to take ownership of the finished product as well."

Brangot looked between Diotitus and Gerard and could see and sense a sudden rise in desire in his friend. He nodded to Gerard and said, "We can assign those tasks when we have a better understanding of the requirements."

Gerard appeared want to argue, but said nothing on that subject. He smiled warmly, albeit a forced smile, and said "Excellent. You may direct any requests for admission to a specific afterworld to me, and I'll try to get it approved. Make sure to list the person or persons you intend to meet."

"Do you have a suggestion on where we should start?" Brangot asked.

"I'd start with Tif," Gerard replied. The god excused himself to attend other matters, leaving Brangot and Diotitus alone.

The two men decided to return home, and left the tower and walked to the Spirit Channel station. The trip to the station was much shorter, and they walked in silence.

They rested at the station, waiting for the next Spirit Channel to arrive.

Brangot looked intently at Diotitus, and said in a reserved tone. "During my In-Life, we had many enemies. This," he hefted the cylindrical weapon with his lower arms, "was the greatest weapon my people ever devised."

Diotitus nodded, and though he had heard most of Brangot's stories, he could tell Brangot was more conversational with his reflections than usual. And, if the moment of insight he experienced in the Conservatory's conference room was to come to fruition, he thought they would need to become closer friends than they ever had over the previous thousands of years.

"It is marvelous in its simplicity," he went on. "It may be used on its own, or its power may be increased by compounding multiple weapons together." Brangot's thick, bark skin made it difficult for him to show subtle emotions, but Diotitus was able to read those subtleties in Brangot's eyes. "One of our greatest victories was over an entire armada of space-faring warships, and the fleet was decimated primarily with this one model of weapon."

"But," Brangot continued, "although diplomacy and negotiations may be encouraged with appropriately metered force, I have been witness to their use with greater effect than the weapon I now hold." He looked thoughtfully at Diotitus, and his eyes were glassy with the memory of a deep and unforgettable wound.

"Over the countless, perhaps infinite, number of years when we have been neighbors in Oblivion, I have known you to have a good heart." Then, his brows furrowed and his expression and tone became angry. "But that academic god," and he jabbed the tip of his weapon in the direction of the tower, "spoke nothing more than academic deceit."

Brangot turned the jutting tip of the weapon down and planted it on the station's wood planked floor, creating a sharp echo. "Tell me plainly, my friend, what deceit did you hear and see, and what deceits did you concoct, in that god's lair?"

Diotitus set his baton and shield down on a station bench and looked up at Brangot. "Do you think this is the best time and place to have this discussion?"

"Let him listen if he can," Brangot said acidly. "The Sprit Channel station is technically an extension of its own afterworld, and I surmise his power stops at the door."

Diotitus nodded in agreement. "Maybe. I'll tell you what I was thinking either way. Gerard, and, I suppose, all of the other Conservatory gods, want to control us. If we followed Gerard's suggestions, we would have to go through him to get approval to enter other afterworlds and tell him with whom we would be in contact. Assuming we could finish Tif's thought, and were we to follow Gerard's suggestion, we would turn the work over to the machine-people who manage the Time Stream. I didn't feel as though rousing Tif would actually matter to them, and perhaps we couldn't rouse her if we spent the remainder of our infinite years trying. I thought of it as a distraction. We finish the first part, and try to wake up Tif to finish the second, but maybe they have already finished the second and only need us to do the first. We would then waste time on Tif, but they would already have what they wanted. Maybe I'm being too conspiratorial, but I think he was deliberately misleading."

Brangot nodded in partial agreement.

"To be honest," Diotitus continued, "Primarily I was wondering what was in it for us. Maybe we can wake up Tif, and that would be great. But that wouldn't mean she would change her mind," and he paused looking away from Brangot for a moment. "She never had romantic feelings for me," Diotitus said sullenly. "I don't believe anything I do would ever change her heart about how she feels. Though, she is a dear friend to the both of us, and it would be nice to be able to rouse her from her present state of mind. I don't consider Tif a reward," and he shook his head. "She is our friend, not a prize. Besides, the Conservatory gods aren't able to help. So, what benefit would we get out of this? We wouldn't be saved by any particular god, and the only ones who would benefit are Gerard and his academic friends."

"Did you have something else in mind?" Brangot asked.

Diotitus smiled fiercely. "We complete Tif's thought," he said in earnest, "without any help from Gerard. We find out what we can about this upcoming Grand Disaster, which afterworlds it will affect, and we make sure we are the only ones who are able and knowledgeable to operate whatever device we concoct. We find out the secrets of Creation Mathematics."

"Ah," Brangot mused, "But the objective may be for the Conservatory to learn about these very things instead of some theoretical device. Perhaps all they are interested in is the truth about this Grand Disaster, or the secrets of Creation Mathematics."

"Maybe," Diotitus admitted. "Therefore, we would have to maintain the secret. Either way, if we do create this device, then we have something of great value to all of the afterworlds."

Brangot listened quietly.

And Diotitus' eyes sparkled, "Brangot, this is like discovering an extremely lucrative mine. All we have to do is work the mine ourselves, and not for them."

"Ah," Brangot at last realized, "I understand. At the moment, we are of no consequence to any afterlife. With this theoretical device, we would be able to provide a very desirable service."

"Yes," Diotitus said.

"Where do you think we should start?" Brangot asked.

"Since we don't have anything, we should start at the beginning," Diotitus answered. "We need to find out the secret of Creation Mathematics."

"And?" Brangot asked.

"I think I know where to look, and my grandfathered status as a god might get us a day-pass."

"Where?" Brangot asked, now growing impatient.

"The afterworld reserved for gods."

BRANGOT, DIOTITUS, AND DOBER JUNG

When Brangot and Diotitus were ready to leave the Conservatory, the Spirit Channel materialized at the station. An agent, this time a machine-person, beckoned them to board. "Spirit Channel to Oblivion now boarding," it called.

Diotitus and Brangot approached the agent. "We were hoping to change destinations," Diotitus told the agent.

"Your schedule is specific for a single round-trip between the Conservatory and Oblivion," the agent said.

Brangot loudly tapped his foot. "Then rebook it," he said, letting his annoyance get the best of his demeanor.

"Where were you hoping to go?" the agent asked irritably.

"The afterworld of gods," Diotitus said. "Afterworld eighteen, or eighteen A, I think."

"Eighteen is Bliss, and eighteen, adjunct A, is the mock-afterworld, Bliss Whip," the agent explained, though was apparently amused thinking about it, and its mood lightened. "That's one strange afterworld. The Tribold sect's god's idea of a joke, before the afterworld restrictions took effect."

"And the afterworld of gods?" Diotitus asked. "Nineteen?"

"Damnation," the agent responded. "The one you're looking for is in administrative afterworld fifteen, adjunct D. Since there is no observation level, you can only enter by appointment and if you were made a god by worship. A god degree is not counted there. It's a very cliquish afterworld."

The agent waited for a moment, then asked, "Am I to take it you're a god?"

Diotitus bowed. "Check your records. I'm filed under

Earth, Greek gods, Appendix J, section two, titled Exceptions."

"Er," the agent said, this time making a whirring noise. "I'm not sure that counts."

"He's a god by worship," Brangot said, "which was the only condition you mentioned."

"The only condition besides being invited," the agent corrected.

"At least ask," Diotitus said. "I need to meet with the god who manages Creation Mathematics."

The agent looked incredulously at Diotitus. "Alright, I'll ask. But if they get annoyed for being bothered, I'm blaming you." The agent consulted a small hand-held computer and spoke in a machine-people dialect. After some time, the agent looked up with a surprised expression. "You've been granted a two-hour pass to meet with Dober Jung."

Brangot and Diotitus were directed to board the Spirit Channel. "After two hours, you will be automatically relocated directly to the Spirit Channel scheduled for Oblivion."

Brangot and Diotitus boarded the Spirit Channel, and headed towards the afterworld of gods.

As they rode, Brangot asked, "Haven't you ever tried to enter an afterworld before now?"

"I used to try all the time with the old delivery service. However, no afterworld would approve a temporary pass because the facilities to automatically kick the soul out didn't exist until the Spirit Channel. Anyway, I guess that is why all the afterworlds said no. I think I tried all of them, even the Hell pits and Damnation."

"Do you really think this Dober Jung is going to give use any details about Creation Mathematics?" Brangot asked.

Diotitus shook his head. "No. All I'm interested in is

the name. If we can get elementary schooling on Creation Mathematics and find out who invented it, then I have an idea on how to get the rest of the details."

"And that is?" Brangot asked.

But Diotitus shook his head. "I don't think it is wise to talk about it right now."

When the Spirit Channel delivered Brangot and Diotitus to afterworld fifteen, adjunct D, a scruffy god was waiting at the station to greet them.

"I'm Dober Jung," he said. "Gerard said you would be stopping by. I can't help you, though, and wanted to be courteous about it rather than refusing your request without a visit."

"He didn't waste any time," Brangot said thoughtfully.

"We were wondering if you could tell us more about Creation Mathematics," Diotitus said, skillfully playing a naïve soul. "Though we had hoped you might leave us with some information to work with, neither of us knows if Creation Mathematics is what we really need."

Dober Jung shrugged. "It's quite simple. I invented a highly evolved set of theories and algorithms for creating and interpreting DNA sequences. At this point in the universe, there are many intelligent civilizations that can decode most portions of a DNA sequence. What they are missing is the equation to create the DNA sequence from a complex set of data."

"I thought that algorithm was known to In-Life species," Brangot remarked.

"It's known now. I planted some of the theories in select individuals belonging to certain species in order to introduce it. It was encrypted in such a way that no one is able to decode it, but anyone may use it." Dober Jung made a crooked smile. "The equation is necessary for time travel, and the gods desired certain civilizations to develop said technology."

"Could we use the encrypted version?" Brangot asked.

Dober Jung shook his head. "Based on what Gerard told me, and assuming his information was accurate, you'll need the unencrypted algorithms, which, as I said, I am unable to give you."

"Out of curiosity, what did Gerard tell you?" Diotitus asked.

"Same thing he told you, I imagine. Same thing all the gods have been told. All time lines are being recycled in order to delay a Grand Disaster which will destroy many afterworlds, including this one and the Conservatory." Dober Jung showed little emotion as he described the possible end of the afterworlds.

"And Oblivion?" Brangot asked.

"Oblivion cannot be destroyed," Dober Jung answered. "Gerard told you the Grand Disaster affected the afterlife, right?"

Diotitus nodded, though glanced at Brangot. "Yes. We wanted to compare notes. All afterworlds are in danger, and they need Tif's idea to save them."

Dober Jung squinted and fell silent while considering his answer. "I think there is a disconnect here. Tif only knows part of the solution, and Gerard, you, and most recently myself, are aware of her idea. Another principle part of the solution will be communal between the three of you, and then you will be able to act on Tif's idea to solve the problem."

"The problem of souls," Brangot tested.

"I'm not sure how Gerard described the problem, but it's not really a secret between the gods." He winked at Diotitus, evidently pleased at slipping in the abrasive joke.

"When your kinsmen," he motioned towards Brangot,

"move to invade afterworlds two hundred ninety nine through three hundred two, they will not be able to pass through Oblivion itself, and will tear through every afterworld, starting with afterworld number one, which is where the soul delivery service once operated, and is currently used by the Spirit Channel."

Diotitus looked questioningly at Brangot. "Those are the human afterworlds. What would they want with those?"

Dober Jung smiled slightly and motioned towards Brangot to wait for his response. "You're asking about a rather ugly affair in the history of afterworlds. The human gods wanted to expand their afterworlds, but the administration wouldn't grant them additional space. Not that they needed it since they had access to the infinite amount of space in afterworld Seventeen, which is the Void, and in their own infinite void, afterworld Seventeen adjunct A, which is Limbo. The Void and Limbo are very limited versions of Oblivion, and the gods can control them. You need extra room, plan accordingly and build in one of those areas."

"But, the humans didn't want to build there?" Diotitus asked.

Dober Jung motioned to Brangot.

Brangot shivered and shook his head. "No, the human gods wanted to keep their Limbo a complete void to ensure that anyone in the void would not be aware anything else existed. My world was in another dimension."

"An unreal world," Dober Jung interjected. "A universe spawned of a universe, and which seems utterly fantastic to the parent universe. In his case," Dober Jung indicated Brangot, "his unreal universe was spawned from the universe that includes humans."

"The human gods, who had some power over their own

In-Life universe, were able to tap into our universe and started extending their afterworlds into it. Eventually, the entire universe from whence my people came was consumed. My people, only aware that humans were responsible, but not aware they were humans of the afterworlds, fought back." Brangot said and then fell quiet.

"They started an In-Life war with humans, and the Earth was destroyed," Dober Jung whispered.

"What?" Diotitus cried and turned to face Brangot. "You blew up the Earth?"

"Have you been living in a hole for the last hundred thousand years?" Dober Jung asked. "It's old news. Besides, the humans blew up their own planet. They were very underhanded in their diplomacy, his still nameless race destroyed Earth's entire fleet of warships, and humans accidentally blew up their own planet."

Diotitus shook his head. "The story you told me was about humans?" He asked Brangot.

Brangot nodded solemnly. "You understand why my kind never talk about it. It's not like any After-Life humans would believe their heavens and hells were stealing space and planets from our universe."

"No long-term harm done," Dober Jung said to Diotitus. "Humans colonized many parts of the universe, and the destruction of Earth and the fleet was only a temporary set back. Brangot's people colonized a few galaxies in the human universe, and all was well."

Diotitus grew angry, but then found himself remarkably dispassionate about it. "So, why are they now coming into the afterlife if they got satisfaction from the Earth being destroyed."

"Ah," Dober Jung said, "there's the rub. They didn't get

satisfaction precisely because the Earth was destroyed, and the humans' underhanded diplomacy tactics only exasperated the situation. In all fairness, the In-Life humans had no idea why Brangot's people were upset. Humans haven't had any real contact with their afterworlds or with their gods for many years. However, there are some gods who believe Brangot's people have since been manipulated, or are being misrepresented, by an insidious foe who seeks to claim Oblivion itself."

"It seems like a long time to carry a grudge," Diotitus said.

"Yes," Dober Jung agreed, "which is one reason why some of the gods don't think Brangot's species is responsible, if involved at all. Operating on future trends is a gray area, so it's all circumspect."

"And how is tracking pieces of souls going to make one shred of difference?" Diotitus asked. "If they're going to destroy the afterworlds, the various bits of soul will wind up in Oblivion, but there won't be an afterworld to claim them"

"That is why the Time Stream is so important. If someone could detect and track every particle during a Grand Disaster, then such a process could be used to reassemble the particles immediately following the disaster." Dober Jung looked at Brangot.

And Brangot spoke softly, "Making the afterworlds invulnerable against an attack."

"Precisely," Dober Jung said.

"So this has nothing to do with souls and worship counts at all," Diotitus said. "There shouldn't be any problems going on a short-reincarnation tour as a worship-whacker, trying to convert as many worshippers as possible. Because the souls don't matter at all. The gods are covering their own asses!"

Dober Jung shrugged. "That's one way of putting it. Of course, eventually, the assailants in this Grand Disaster will find their way into Oblivion and destroy everything there as well. Granted, Oblivion itself is safe from harm, but everything in Oblivion is fair game."

"Can they destroy the Time Stream?" Brangot asked.

"They can try," Dober Jung said ruefully. "You really must visit the Time Stream to fully appreciate how well the machine-people have managed it. There are many filters and by-ways built around the stream. The Stream itself is absolutely invulnerable, the same way Oblivion is invulnerable. However, the inhabitants of Oblivion do not share in the same protection. And, if the filters are destroyed, or changed, then a lot of bad things will start to happen. Paradoxes caused by time travel would not be caught and would take on a permanent effect. One day you wake up and discover you never existed. And that's a weird feeling. Experienced it myself a few times in the early days."

"So why don't you tell us the algorithms to Creation Mathematics so we can make this stupid thing, whatever it is supposed to be, and defend the afterworlds?" Diotitus asked angrily.

"Because," Dober Jung said, "the one thing I'm sure you have in the back of your head, and something I certainly know Gerard wouldn't tell you, is the moment you create this device and connect it to the Time Stream, you will be the most powerful entities in any place, in any time."

"Probably why Gerard wanted us to tell him everything," Brangot said sullenly, still smarting from the disclosure of his people's history with humans.

Dober Jung shrugged. "Everyone has their own agenda."

"So, you're not going to tell us the algorithms?" Diotitus asked again.

Dober Jung shook his head. "I cannot make that decision by myself. Because of the nature of the information, it is the decision of many, many gods, and they do not think it is a necessary component of the solution."

"Then why did Gerard say it was?" Diotitus asked.

"I'm not sure," Dober Jung replied. "Why do you think Gerard thought to speak with me before you arrived?"

Their pass expired, and Brangot and Diotitus did not have a chance to thank Dober Jung for the information. Instead, they found themselves on the Spirit Channel headed for Oblivion.

PARTICLE LINE

Metallic ribbons intertwining, splitting and splintering, fusing and twisting, were the foundation of the Time Stream. The ribbons were small and finely crafted, and had the viscosity and weight of syrup. Some believed touching the streams of time produced an electrically charged vibration that was the soul of all that ever was and all that may be. A few believed the Time Stream itself was a god.

The machine-people who administered the Time Stream, and therefore time itself, knew otherwise. Their description of the Time Stream was decidedly vague but included the noteworthy point that it was not the construct of a god, for one could trace the Time Stream back to the birth or first appearance of any god. Those portions of the Time Stream were encrypted and protected from public purview.

With permission from the machine-people to perform a data acquisition test in the Time Stream, Brangot watched as

Diotitus reviewed his own hand-scribbled notes taken during a brief meeting with the machine-people earlier in the day. The two spoke excitedly over the previous day about how to build a device to track every particle in the known and unknown universe using the Time Stream, but there was still tension over the revelation that Brangot's people had been at war with the humans. There was also a more overt tension; neither really knew what they were doing.

Diotitus set his notes down and looked up at Brangot with a serious and drawn face. He felt tired from sitting through the meeting with the machine-people earlier in the day, and realized he had not been to his apartment nor slept in more than three days. "Brangot, look, I don't really feel one way or the other about what went on between your people and humans. It would have been nice if you had told me, but I guess I understand your reservations."

Brangot felt some relief and nodded. The slightest of smiles crossed his lips. "It was a difficult time for my people. But were I to answer your question regarding my home world and I pointed to human Heaven and said, there, my home world once existed where human heaven now stands, I think it would have been hard to accept."

Diotitus nodded. "I wanted you to know there were no hard feelings coming from this side of the Time Stream." He smiled and looked down at the stream.

"Are you ready to tell me how you plan on finding the secret to Creation Mathematics?" Brangot asked, for Diotitus had been very reserved about it.

"No, sorry," he apologized. "If I give any hint or indication, the gods will pick up on it. Even if they can't pick up on it here, I'm sure the machine-people would. I suppose it's really a simple thing."

Diotitus smirked and cocked his head. "You know, I think I'm starting to spew the same babble Tif was saying."

Brangot shrugged. "May I be of any help then?"

Diotitus nodded. "Yes. I hope you were listening better than I was this morning. We need to create a by-pass, so I have the by-pass module here," and he held up what resembled a simple, bent pipe. "We need two time filters, two entity filters, and two engram filters." He held up three different sets of small disks.

"Those look like they would be the ones," Brangot said. "They're clearly marked, anyway. Is this going to cause any problems?"

Diotitus shook his head. "These are beginner filters and have some sort of built-in safeguards against creating a paradox, and they won't allow us to make any changes affecting a time line."

"I suppose all I need to do," Diotitus started, "is add the by-pass to the Time Stream." He touched one end of the bent-pipe to the Time Stream, and it remained in place even as the metallic ribbons representing time flowed around it. "Next, we add a filter for a specific person at a specific time," he continued, and affixed two of the filters to one end of the by-pass. He paused, and then after some thought, turned the pipe around so the filtered end was in the stream. "Add the same to the other end," and he affixed the other set of filters to the opposite end. "And, now, the really clever part." He added one engram filter to each end of the pipe, and then pushed the by-pass fully into the Time Stream.

"What now?" Brangot asked.

Diotitus shrugged. "I have no idea." He picked up the by-pass and turned it over in his hands, examining the engram filters on each end. He narrowed his eyes, searching for some indication of change, and then removed one of the en-gram filters and set the by-pass down on the ground. Excited silence overwhelmed him and he held up the filter for Brangot to see. "A bit horrific how simple that was," he said.

Brangot scrunched his eyebrows down and pursed his lips. "You mean?" he started, but didn't fully articulate the question.

"Next, we need to construct the device," Diotitus said.

"The machine-people have equipment to automatically construct tools and other machines for working with the Time Stream," Brangot said. "I suppose we could solicit their help. What else remains?"

"We need to figure out where to store so much data, and how to access it," Diotitus said. "And I wonder if the answer is the idea we are supposed to share with Tif. So, we can ask the machine-people to help build the device, we can add in the contents of the engram filter, and then we can concentrate on Tif."

The machine-people were very receptive to helping Diotitus and Brangot build their custom filters for the Time Stream, and a device for controlling the filters. The two men had the impression the machine-people were glad someone took an interest in their work, though Brangot was very wary of the motivations. In less than four hours, the majority of their device was finished by many thousands of small spider-legged machine-helpers. Their spherical white bodies and cartoon-like legs moved quickly and responded to everything from abstract thought to specific details. At one point, one of the bots simply took the engram filter from Diotitus. He didn't think to voice his concern, though hoped that if the machine-people were aware of the contents they would keep the infor-mation to themselves.

"It's amazing," Brangot remarked while the device was constructed. "I'm amazed we've lasted this long."

"What do you mean?" Diotitus asked.

"Look," and he gestured with all four arms and hands to the thousands of machine-helpers working on their device. "We haven't been saved, yet we are able to build complex things with only a thought."

"This one time," Diotitus said. "It's not as though the machine-people might let us use their facilities again, or anyone else for that matter."

"Not only the device, but everything in Oblivion. If we had been saved, how would another afterworld better suit us? Beyond the pleasantries of color and, I imagine, the requisite devotion to one or more gods, it seems to me that we may partake in many of the same benefits of the saved."

"Speak for yourself," Diotitus said half-jokingly, then amended, "but I get what you're saying. Anyway, why do you think it is amazing we have lasted so long?"

"Our every vice, active or lethargic, overfed and over-consumed, for eternity. I'm amazed we haven't become Droolers ourselves. We've spent so much time in Oblivion and yet what do we really know about it? We only see its fruits and its boundaries, but not the place itself." He watched as the machine-helpers went about their work. "I've been to the Time Stream countless times, and have conversed with the machine-people on many occasions. I know their names, their various expression and models, their entire histories. But I never bothered to ask them what they do here besides making idle chit-chat or framing exploratory questions for which I have no genuine interest in the answer. I may have thought I was interested, but I wonder if I have only been existing to pass the the time. Have you ever considered if a

Drooler gave up on their on existence because they felt the same way, passing the time with no worthwhile pursuit?" Brangot continued to watch the machine-helpers as they fashioned new filters and polished the casings for the device. "I'm amazed because in these last few days I have realized I stopped trying to discover myself as I had tried to do in life. Perhaps ever since the first day of my After-Life, I stopped trying to better myself. I have simply existed and simply consumed, grossly gorged and grossly fasted, mindlessly wandered and emotionlessly fornicated, and all for what? To try to grow, or to hide who I am?"

Diotitus nodded slightly. "I suppose I'm confused. Since the gods never made themselves available or approachable, I never knew what to expect. But now that I've met them, it doesn't seem any different than what I remember from life."

Diotitus looked at his hands, a bitter thought crossing his mind, and then he looked up at Brangot. "Do you still feel like the same person you were when you died?"

Brangot smiled lamely. "You do realize we have this conversation at least once a year."

"But it seems different now," Diotitus said. "I always thought of Oblivion as a dark and forgotten corner in the After-Life, and not a place where all afterworlds are joined."

The machine-helpers had stopped moving and retreated to the edges of the workshop floor. In the center was a metallic primary-blue shaded cube, precisely two meters on all sides. All sides were flat and featureless, except one that held two screens, several complicated controls, and an array of detachable filters for the Time Stream. Several connections were identified for data storage. With the exception of where the data would be stored, the device appeared to be entirely self-contained and sealed.

"What would prevent someone from coming along and taking the whole device?" Diotitus asked.

Three machine-helpers scurried across the floor, and each dropped a large, unique key at Diotitus' and Brangot's feet, and then scurried away. The first key was shaped like a palm-sized obelisk and was colored flat, primary-green. Brangot's name was etched in heavy block print on each side of the key. The second key was shaped to fit over the first key, was colored flat, primary-yellow, and bore Diotitus' name. The third key was torus-shaped, it's interior was cut to fit the base of the first key, and its anterior was shaped to fit inside a beveled portion of the second key. The third key bore Tif's name.

Diotitus crouched, picked up the keys, and passed Brangot's to his friend's awaiting palm, and then offered him Tif's. "You should hold onto hers."

"Assuming these keys are of significant worth, previous romantic involvement shouldn't dictate who is the more responsible to safeguard Tif's key." Brangot gently pushed Tif's key back. "I think it is precisely because you're relationship with Tif is not complicated by romantic relations that you should hold it until she is ready to take it."

Diotitus smiled at his friend. "If we can't wake up Tif, these won't really matter."

A machine-person approached from the hallway and entered the workshop. "Pardon the interruption."

Both men turned to see a machine-person they had not met before.

"I see your device has been constructed and suitably safeguarded." The machine-person walked around the device and then inspected the keys. It then extended a humanoid hand to Brangot, who shook it, and then Diotitus, who did likewise. "My name is Moto."

Diotitus and Brangot introduced themselves, however, they felt sure Moto already knew their names.

"I was quite impressed with your recovery of the Creation Mathematics algorithms," Moto said to Diotitus. "I admit to being surprised when souls from more primitive eras are able to work with more complicated and technical processes."

Diotitus wasn't sure how to take Moto's remark, and said, "Thanks, I think. It didn't seem that hard. You've made it easy to work with the Time Stream, and your helpers did all of the work. We only thought about what we wanted."

Moto's smoothly cut and narrow silver lips twisted into a knowing smile. "Knowing what you want is sometimes all that matters. With our permission, any soul may have used our facilities to fabricate any number of simple or complex items, but only the two of you, and your absent friend, thought to make this." It gestured to the device with a delicately crafted arm.

"But, we were told to make it," Brangot said uncertainly. "Tif had an idea, the gods somehow found out about it, and then they asked us to finish the idea. We may as well have followed a trail of bread crumbs."

Moto continued to smile. "When is any idea or creation not at the end of a carefully lain trail? Every scrap of insight, each mental faculty that brings distinction to abstract thought; these all contribute to the trail."

"I think the gods contributed more than a few scraps information," Brangot said.

"Yet, the device in this room came from your minds, not theirs," Moto contested. "And," it continued, "The gods have their own means to quickly construct technologically advanced products. It would have been a simple matter for any god to create this, and having direct access to the Time Stream could have been arranged."

"Then, why didn't Gerard, or any one of the gods, create the device?" Diotitus asked. "They sounded as though they knew what it was supposed to do."

"Knowing what needs to be done and visualizing a means to meet that need are two different skills." Moto looked between Diotitus and Brangot. "In all of your years living in Oblivion, you have managed to gain new skills and acquire new information. However, and I apologize for inadvertently overhearing your earlier conversation, you have continued to live the life of who you were, and not the life of who you are. You do not realize that you are capable of at least grasping basic technological advances that are now a part of your life, and which may not have been invented in your In-Life. If I were to succinctly describe the difference between the two of you and Gerard, as well as many other gods, it would be that they simply lacked the creativity to visualize this type of solution. Our involvement," and it gestured to the facilities and machine-helpers, "Only expedited construction."

Diotitus and Brangot listened without interrupting the machine.

Moto continued after a momentary pause, "You were right to be careful about the acquisition of the formulas, and I want you to know its implementation is at least as equally secure in the device as the original."

Diotitus smiled slightly. "Thank you."

Moto glanced at Brangot and went on, "it wouldn't do any harm to give you more details. The Time Stream isn't merely a representation of time. It is every particle in every universe over time, adequately represented by intertwining streams. One can filter and alter those streams, though we take great pains to prevent anything that might alter the events of any time line. Diotitus thought to give a name to the original idea that would blossom into Creation Mathematics, and implant the name in Dober Jung's mind in the past. While making a slight alteration in time, it was ultimately an insignificant one because the time line was in no way altered. Diotitus was then able to extract the information by searching for the name in the particles of the Time Stream related to Jung's memories."

"Very ingenious," Brangot admitted. "But isn't it dangerous if you allow anyone to make even the slightest change to the Time Stream?"

Moto nodded. "Yes. However, I was fully aware why you were here and of the impending Grand Disaster. After all, we administer the Time Stream and the gods may not recycle periods of time without our involvement."

"About the Grand Disaster and the Time Stream," Moto continued, "I wanted to pass along some small bit of information that was made known to me within the last hour. The majority of gods have ruled there is not enough evidence to confirm a Grand Disaster will occur, and they have voted for time to move forward."

Brangot looked at Moto with noticeable concern. "Were our efforts for nothing?"

"On the contrary, whether a Grand Disaster does occur, I believe you will find great reward in what you have accomplished." Moto glanced about the room, "and I hope you will not forget our assistance."

"How could we forget?" Diotitus asked. "Without your help we wouldn't have been able to start."

"About the decision, I wanted to let you know so as to impress upon you the importance of completing the device.

If the Grand Disaster does come about, you must be ready."

"When will time move forward?" Brangot asked.

"It has already started," Moto replied.

MYRRH DESERT PARK

The Grand Disaster had set in on the afterworlds within hours of time moving forwards, around the same time that Brangot and Diotitus had made their way from the Time Stream to Myrrh Desert Park. From what they had been told, the enemy was not Brangot's race as they had been led to believe. The invaders were an unreal construct from a universe spawned within a chasm between afterworld three hundred one, adjunct Z, a human Christian spin-off afterworld, and three hundred two, a Mormon afterworld. They were able to break into afterworld one when the Spirit Channel inadvertently crossed over the newly formed chasm. Eventually, the invasion would be classified as an error in logistics and inadequate planning by the Spirit Channel administration.

As far as Diotitus and Brangot knew, the invading force was still working its way through the administration afterworlds. Diotitus thought the invaders would be inevitably held up in afterworld fifteen, adjunct D, the afterworld of gods, at least for a few hours.

For their part, they had been frantically trying to rouse Tif. She was still a Drooler in Myrrh Desert Park, and they desperately needed her to wake up so they could come to some conclusion about how to store the particle data. Then, they could turn on the device and make the afterworlds invulnerable to attack by directly controlling events in time through the Time Stream, using the device to track and recreate complex structures such as souls or entire afterworlds.

"Tif," Brangot said in earnest and deposited the key inscribed with her name on her lap. "Wake up, Tif!" he said loudly.

Helpful pedestrians were warned away by both Diotitus' and Brangot's swift and forceful reactions whenever someone tried to explain she was a Drooler.

"Tif," Diotitus said loudly, "It's me, Diotitus." He took her hand in his, and then placed it on the key in her lap. "Tif, can you feel this? It's what you were thinking about. Brangot and I made it." He didn't bother to mention the machine-helpers did all of the heavy lifting.

Brangot kneeled next to her and placed his leafy and knotted fingers on her knee. "Tif," he spoke her name again. "It's important to everyone that you wake up."

But she offered no response.

"She's can't hear us!" Diotitus said angrily. "She doesn't want to hear us. Oblivion will fall around her and she is content to stare into a …" and then he paused.

Brangot and Diotitus, each holding one of Tif's hands, looked at the other, both sharing in a communal thought.

"The chasm," Diotitus started, thinking about where the invading force had originated. "Presumably near-infinite."

"With instantaneous access through the Spirit Channel," Brangot concluded. He wrinkled his brow and remarked, "Very strange. It now seems so obvious and clear."

"So simple," Diotitus added.

Diotitus felt his eyes water and he firmly gripped Tif's hand. Looking into Tif's vacant eyes, searching for a spark of recognition, he whispered, "Dober Jung said we would be together when we shared the thought, but he never said whether Tif would be awake."

Brangot touched Diotitus' shoulder and tipped his head away from the Obsidian Sea, which bordered one side of Myrrh Desert Park. "She will still be here," he spoke in a voice of excitement and sympathy. He stood and gently pulled Diotitus to his feet. "But, we must hurry."

Diotitus looked longingly at Tif, and then the two men raced back to the Time Stream and to the device that would save Oblivion and the afterworlds.

Moto greeted them by asking if Tif was awake.

"No," Diotitus said an a quiet tone, "but we had an idea. We need a place to put all of the information. And, we think we know where we can store it."

"Where?" Moto asked.

"The chasm leading to the invader's universe," Brangot said. "From here, we can tap into the Spirit Channel to move the information."

"Interesting," Moto said thoughtfully. "And by using the Spirit Channel as a conduit, you could have almost immediate access. Let's find out if it will work," he said and then instructed the machine-helpers to connect and activate the device. "You'll need to activate the device with your keys."

Brangot and Diotitus rushed to the device, assembled the three keys, and unlocked the device for use. As soon as it was turned on, they could see the stream of particle information flowing out of Oblivion and towards the universe of the unreal. Brangot configured the device to operate in a Grand Disaster prevention mode by manipulating controls the machine-helpers built based on his thoughts. The device automatically locked down the afterworlds and Oblivion from attack.

With the device activated, the invaders were brought to a stand still, and the gods voted to banish them into Damnation.

Several days following the successful prevention of the invasion, Gerard summoned Brangot and Diotitus to the Conservatory where he expressed uncertainty regarding their failure to follow his recommended guidelines. Gerard told them he had been left out of the decision making process, at which time he presented them with a plan for administering the device. Brangot told Gerard in no uncertain terms it was not any god's decision to make, and the two men left Gerard's hand-written plan on the conference room table when they left.

After their follow-up meeting with Gerard, Brangot and Diotitus met with Dober Jung. Dober Jung expressed interest in how the men had figured out Creation Mathematics, admitting that the information was given to him from an unseen presence, and his role was to encrypt the algorithms; he was never consciously aware of the unencrypted equations. Diotitus didn't understand the wickedly complex equations extracted from Dober Jung's memories using the Time Stream, and felt he was honest in saying they never solved that particular problem.

In the ensuing years, Brangot and Diotitus worked with Moto and Dober Jung, and occasionally with gods from other afterworlds. They organized research programs with Conservatory graduates, and helped restore souls that were scattered in the wake of Grand Disasters. Acting as administrators to the device built from Tif's last burst of insight, they weren't gifted with god-like powers or anything beyond some limited influence and passing recognition. Many souls would never know that their arrival in some afterworld with their entire soul intact, whether the afterworld was a heaven, hell, nirvana, or reincarnation, was due to a one time Greek god named Diotitus, and a chlorophyll-skinned warrior named Brangot.

As for Tif, Diotitus held vigil for her every night. He hoped she would realize she could be productive in an eternal life. It was not until those few frantic days when both Brangot and Diotitus discovered life does not stop in the hereafter. It had been so easy to over-indulge their vices and to let themselves be content with the people they were, and be blind to the people they had become. Diotitus prayed to the original fire-and-brimstone Gods, hoping a moment of inspiration might come enabling him to rouse Tif from her state of mind. Until then, he kept watch over his friend, and discovered a purpose to his After-Life so he may never again lose himself in Oblivion.

Just Sing
Tracy Crowe

There's nobody here
There's nobody watching
Just let the
Tears fall down
And the sobs
Shake you
In the presence
Of the Spirit

In the darkness
Before the light
The songbird knows
Without faith
Or intellect
That the sun will rise
He is not conscious
He has no voices
Of the past to
Haunt his every dogged
Step

He just sings
>Like there is no one there
>Like he is the only bird around
>Like his song is the best in the world
>Like he doesn't care if tomorrow ever comes

He just sings

So laugh in your quiet place
And cry the great sobs in
Your aching belly
The world is not here to
Pass judgment

Just sing in the darkness
Knowing deep inside
You
That the light will
Will always come.

And Now...Some Fairly Good Truly Horrible Martial Arts Fiction That We'll Call

JUDGE NOT
K.A. Thompson

The sweat glistened off the chiseled, cut edges of muscle, skin gleaming under the lights, droplets of saline cutting through the air as she sliced the atmosphere with a perfect flying sidekick. The resounding crunch as her heel connected with her opponent's nose reverberated off the walls, filling the room with the sick feeling of death, an anticipation of finality, the waiting and expectation of rivers of blood coming first in small drops, rapidly escalating into rivulets of doom, pooling mercilessly on the floor beneath the briskly dying man.

He should have known.

Someone, somewhere, should have warned him.

It was a brisk day, the sort of morning where the sun shines off the drops of dew sitting upon the tips of blades of grass, where breath drifts from children's mouths in wisps of steam, billowing and fading as their shrill voices fill the air with nonsensical laughter. It was a morning filled with the promise of more to come, the minutes slipping quietly into each other, multiplying and mutating to form hours, and the rest of the day. It was a perfect day. A day that would go on.

Mickey the Stump took a long draw off his cigarette, a well aged, compact, Viceroy Slim Filter Tip. He sucked the filter hard, drawing in the acrid, bitter smoke, feeling it sear down his throat, heating and expanding in his chest, filling his lungs with the nicotine and oxygen-robbing carbon monoxide, the pure joy of death packed neatly into little squares of twenty. He sucked until his lungs could take no more, relishing the fire and fetor, knowing down to the very fibers of his soul that to kiss him would be akin to licking an ashtray. Yes, it was a very fine cigarette. The kind he greeted each new day with.

Mickey slowly exhaled, watching himself in the mirror behind the bar, the smoke curling in tendrils out of his nostrils. He flared his nose, and then constricted it, fascinated to see the stream of smoke become little puffs. It popped from his nose and slowly ascended. It was a good way to exercise the proboscis, he told himself. A good way indeed. "You never know," he sighed, "when you'll need a strong hard nose to kill a man. A chiseled nose. A big nose."

Mickey the Stump stared at his nose in the mirror. None better. None finer. None so big. You could drive a truck into Mickey's nose. Maybe even turn around.

He fixated his gaze past his own reflection, staring at the image of the bar door as it creaked open slowly, gingerly, revealing a stream of light in dots of sunrays and dust motes. Then she stepped in. He was captivated. The ash dropped from the tip of his cigarette into his lap. He never blinked. It didn't matter. He was Mickey the Stump, and that was why he was Mickey the Stump.

She was a gorgeous woman, and tall. He turned on his barstool to get a better look at her, glorifying in the finely tuned muscles pulsating beneath her Wrangler Cowboy Cut Denim Jeans, the pull and thrust of her thighs, the quads so acutely developed…he wondered, drawing on the last vestiges of his cigarette, how many men she had snapped in two with those legs.

Mickey felt the blood rush in his head as she sat on the stool beside him, hearing the torrent of corpuscles and leukocytes surge in mighty pulsations through his arteries and veins, and he knew she wanted him. He could feel the strong vibrations emanating from the woman. She was his. And her nose was mighty fine.

He lit another Viceroy Slim Filter Tipped, and drew in a hard breath. She was watching each movement, from the flick of his Bic to the end of the cigarette touching his lips. He saw the draw of her lips in a smile, the glint in her eyes. As she lifted her hand, he knew. She wanted him. They were made for each other.

Mickey the Stump closed his eyes for just a moment, savoring the anticipation of a lifetime with the woman of his dreams, savoring the flavor of his Viceroy, tasting the grim edge in the wisp and grayish smoke, telling himself that if the lifetime didn't stand before him, a few hours would do him a world of good.

Mickey the Stump woke hours later, his teeth covered with the mash of his Viceroy Slim Filtered Tipped, his well exercised and muscled nose caked with dried blood and skewed to one side. He blinked, waiting to feel the pain, the searing agony, the certain knowledge that he was alive and would have preferred to have been dead. As his vision cleared he saw the sign on the mirror at the bar. NO SMOKING.

He spit the final vestiges of tobacco and cotton filter from his mouth, wondering why and how, and who.

The bartender merely shrugged. She had left hours ago, leaving Mickey the Stump to contemplate why and how, and most of all, who the woman was. She was a strong woman, and he was impressed.

It was the bullet that had Detective Timothy Tate, Old Tim, worried the most. It was a beautiful bullet, gold and softly tipped, shining as it nestled there in the palm of his hand, warm from the spit of Hobo Joe's lips. It was a bullet unbesmerched by the ragged lines and scratches of the Ruger Mark III .22 it should have been fired from. It was thin and delicate the way a .22 should be. Unsullied by hammering of a gun stop, it nestled there in Hobo Joe's teeth, gleaming until Old Tim pried it loose with his fingernails.

Hobo Joe smiled, the hole carved between his teeth perfect and round, so perfect Old Tim knew he could slide his pencil in there and have it stick without wobbling. "She was beautiful," Hobo Joe muttered. "An Amazon. A goddess sent here to spire me away from my sins and deeds of evil."

Old Tim grunted. "Yeah. And what might they be?"

Hobo Joe shrugged. It didn't matter. She was the perfect vision of loveliness and she had graced his very soul with her touch.

"How'd it get there, Joe?" Old Tim pressed. "This wasn't fired from any handgun I've ever seen."

Hobo Joe shook his head in amazement. It was a sight to behold, nothing he could ever explain. Old Tim would never understand, he hadn't been there, hadn't seen her perfect form glide effortlessly through the air, her foot positioned perfectly, the pierce of her sidekick as it met his mouth, the metal slipping gently between his lips.

Old Tim stared at the .22 bullet in his hand. It should have been a shell, a lifeless, spent and mangled piece of metal, blackened and twisted by the powder that was needed to expel it from the nose of the semiautomatic it was meant to come from.

"Doesn't make any sense, Joe."

"Doesn't have to," Joe sighed. "She don't need a gun, Old Tim. She's got *toes*." Joe leaned back, feeling the hole in his teeth with his tongue, the smooth edges sending an electric shiver through his mouth. He remembered her, all right. And he would never forget.

Old Tim pressed the cold, hard manacles around her wrist slowly, listening to the snap as each ridge of the lock caught, the tick-tick-tick of handcuffs coming together in perfect harmony. It had to be.

He looked at her warily, glancing from eye to eye, trying to read the thoughts simmering in that cauldron of gray matter nestled between her ears.

"Ah, you have to do it, Old Tim," she whispered, her voice throaty, still filled with the phlegm of sleep, the cough of a real Loogie not yet hacked up and spit out. "You know you have to."

Tim let his eyes roam the length of her body. She was right, of course, he had no choice. He reached to the back of his waistband, fumbling for a moment before finding the next set of handcuffs. He bent and slipped each side carefully over an ankle, befuddled by the strength he could feel in her hands and her feet, the full amplitude of power that warned him one wrong move and he could be dead.

"How'd you know, Tim?" she asked in a deep voice. It

was a voice that could haunt a man for years, resonant and filled with the lust and rage and pure venomous femaleness that no real man could resist. "How did you realize?"

Old Tim took a step back from her, carefully considering. "The first one could have been an accident," he surmised aloud, listening to the sound of his own voice. It was a good voice, a sure voice. A voice that had been his since puberty and was carrying him well. "Just a training accident. A man that didn't block and get out of the way.

"Mickey the Stump was just plain stupid. He could have picked any woman in the bar, but instead he picked you, a smoke hating, large nose fearing woman with a quick fist. But Stump appreciates a fast knuckle, fine muscles, and the taste of his own cigarettes. He could have cared less, once he got another drink.

"And Hobo Joe...he was the one who remembered. He was the one who knew who you were and why you did what you did. He remembered them all."

"I had to do it, Tim," she confessed, her voice as sure and strong as her biceps, flexing and taunting until Old Tim was sure her arms and lips would explode. "They screwed my kid, Tim. They got what was coming to them."

"The boy lost fair and square," Tim told her. "And number two ain't half bad."

"He was number one and you know it. He doesn't sleep at night any more, Tim, knowing what those three did, their stupid little score cards hanging in the air for the whole world to see. He should have been First, Tim! I had to do it, I had to revenge him!"

Old Tim shook his head sadly. "There was always next year."

"There's never a next year, Tim. Next year is a new

division, new kids. He was first this year. They took it away from him. And I took it back!" She straightened up proudly, arching her back, chest thrust out hard. "How'd you know it was me, Tim?"

Old Tim reached into his pocket for the .22 bullet. "You shoved this into Hobo Joe's mouth with a kick." He pointed down at her feet. "It takes a certain kind of person to be able to hold a bullet between their toes and hit the mark. Not too many women have your feet."

She stared down at her toes. They were good toes, long and thin and straight. But her second toe was always longer than the first, making it easy to pick things up off the floor and carry them around. Old Tim had seen that from the start. Who else could jam a bullet so hard and so neatly with a foot but a person with a very long second toe?

No one, Tim had concluded. No one at all.

It was a good arrest, the kind of arrest that can make a cop proud, the kind of arrest that makes the papers and collects accolades in every shape and form, from the key to the city down to the kids on the street with their cheery words of admirations and happy smiles as they ride past on their brand new bicycles bought with money from birthdays and Christmases, money that Grandma and Grandpa sent every year without fail, good money, happy money. Old Tim sat back in the squeaky leather chair at his old oak desk, the one he had taken from his grandfather's house years ago, when the old man lost his memory and wouldn't have noticed if the tooth fairy had moved in and begun sleeping in the bed next to him. Yes, it was a good arrest, freeing the streets and easing the minds of men who had heard whispers of the tall woman with the long and well muscled legs, the woman who no man could resist yet every man must.

Old Tim closed the file folder and dropped it into the basket at the side of his desk. It was finished. Concluded. Terminated. Done with. Finito.

The streets were now safe.

Men were now safe.

Tournament judges could now judge freely and without the fear that they would become accosted by *The Karate Mom From Hell*.

The One Dragon: Keyla's Journey
JoEllen Drazan

"You know our laws," refuted Elder Haim, his rasping voice cutting through Elder Myrron's plea. "She is not permitted to travel the path. To even speak of it is blasphemy."

"I tell you, she has the gift. I have seen it in her eyes," Elder Myrron pleaded to the council members. "She has the strongest mind I have seen in many a year and she needs to be trained." Slowly the sacred herbs burned in the fire at the center of the tent. The thick canvas of the tent, painted with the ancient symbols of his people, prevented most of the smoke from escaping. Waiving the acrid smoke away, he looked around the circle of the council. Nine old and worn men held the fate of his adopted daughter. The young orphan girl who had shared his life since her parent's death five years ago. Keyla had just turned ten when the incident had happened.

"Strong or not, I believe it is your heart that she has bewitched," Elder Yumma argued from the shadowed corner of the tent. His bent, withered frame twitching in impatience "There has never been a woman shaman and there never will be. Women do not posses the necessary skills and knowledge to maintain leadership." He thumped his staff on the carpeted ground, emphasizing his words. "It is not allowed. She will not travel the path to see The One Dragon. I do not see the point of bringing it to the floor. The council has better things to discuss than this slip of a girl." The elders nodded, agreeing with Yumma.

Myrron feared that he had pushed the other council members too far. Since the ancient days, no women were shamans. It was law that women were not allowed the privilege of training and meeting the dragon. Still, he did not see a logical reason to prevent women from attempting the paths. Many of the old laws have changed. Some, like this one, remained rooted in ancient lore and myths. He resigned himself to the fact that he would not persuade the elders tonight.

Stubborn old men, He thought to himself as he shifted on the uncomfortable pile of cushions. "I will wait. In a year, the gift in her will be obvious to all of you. It is then that I will readdress the council. I, Elder Myrron, step from the speaker's chair."

"I, Elder Yumma, step to the speaker's chair," Yumma spoke the traditional words of the council, even though there was no physical speaker's chair in the tent. The formality remained. "There has been an increase in the number of attacks from the shadow hounds to our camps. I am concerned on how to better protect our people. Place your suggestions to the floor."

Myrron quickly lost interest in the remaining proceedings of the council. Though this meeting had been called to the Ternel Camp, he had little to do with defenses against the shadow hounds. He was appointed as a Council Elder of the city of Shilrey. The beasts had never attacked the city, its high walls surrounding would prevent them from doing any damage to its residences. In tradition, the council convened once a moon in each of the camps to go over any concerns of the people. Myrron found these sessions to be quite boring. The long discussions on the herding of animals and the seasonal plantings never held his attention. He had enough concerns keeping the city and the tens of thousands of its inhabitants in order.

"Elder Myrron," Yumma said, snapping Myrron out of his reprieve, "is there anything else you wish to bring to the floor?"

"No, Elder Yumma." Myrron replied, wondering if there was something important that he missed while his thoughts had drifted.

"Then I, Elder Yumma, call The Council of the Shilrey concluded." Yumma thumped his staff three times. The elders broke into groups speaking in hushed voices.

"Elder Myrron," Haim said, stopping Myrron with a skeletal hand on his sleeve. "I am concerned about you. This is not the first time you have brought the girl to the council's attention. Are you sure that she has the gift?"

"Yes, Elder Haim. If only the council would put her to the tests then they would see how strong in the gift Keyla is. Until they do, there is nothing I can say that will change their minds." Myrron said shaking his head.

"It is not wise to go against the laws laid down by our ancestors." Haim reminded him.

"Many laws have been changed in the past 400 years since the exodus across the plains. Perhaps, it is time to change one more?" Myrron inquired. Noticing Haim's closed expression, he ceased his efforts. "Do not ask me more unless you are willing to give the girl a chance."

Haim regarded Myrron, his green eyes flaring briefly,

"As you wish, however, I hope you will reconsider pursuing this matter."

Myrron retreated from the whispers in the council tent. Once outside, he breathed deeply of the clean mountain air. Looking up, he realized the council meeting had lasted longer than he anticipated. The second moon was about to show its face in the eastern sky. As quickly as his old legs could take him, Myrron crossed the camp over well-packed dirt trails. It was the largest camp outside the city, a sprawling mass of tents along the Ternel River. Seeing the soft light ahead, he shook his head. He should have known Keyla would be waiting for him. Keyla's dark brown eyes and solemn face already reflected the verdict of the council's decision. The light from the lantern in her hand cast a soft glow upon the path. Opening the flap to the tent, she ducked inside.

Her mind has perceived the emotional currents of the evening. Myrron mused, *If only they would look not at the girl but the strength of the gift she was born with.* In his heart he knew that Keyla was special and someday she would meet The One Dragon. He believed she would become a powerful Shaman, and one of such power that had not been seen since the time of the ancients.

I can see her mind growing and without receiving training she will not be able to control herself when she does meet her. Myrron thought sadly of the boy in one of the other camps who did not receive the proper training. Just over a year ago, he was sent up the mountain paths to see her, The One Dragon. He came back mad. His mind overwhelmed from the touching. Little that was once the young man remained in a shell of a body. He had to be taken care of by the women of the camp, unable to do anything except the simplest of tasks.

Myrron followed Keyla and sat down on a pile of cushions. "You know the answer from tonight's council meeting," he stated without question. "Your mind is growing, child, and soon, they will have no choice but to see how special you are."

"Myrron," Keyla began, pouring tea into small wooden cups, "I know you wish the best for me, but the council is firm. I am just a girl and am of no matter to them." She sighed wistfully, handing a cup of tea to him.

"Just a girl?" Myrron smiled at his charge. "You haven't been 'just a girl' since you were born. Despite what the council has decided, I have made my own choice concerning you."

Keyla glanced up, a frown on her face, "You aren't sending me away are you?"

"No, child, you are not being sent away. Quite the contrary, I will keep you with me and train you myself." Myrron smiled at Keyla's shocked expression.

"Without the council's approval…" she trailed off, slowly excitement dawned upon her face. "How are you going to train me?"

"I will teach you all that I know." Myrron took her small hands in his withered ones. "One day you will face her, my dear. When that time comes the elders will have no choice but to recognize whom you are. You will need to be prepared."

Keyla looked at Myrron with a smile and said, "You have such faith in my destiny and in me. Yet, I am afraid that I will let you down."

"Time will show the truth, don't fret." Myrron patted her hands. "Now it is very late and we have a busy day tomorrow. Time to go to sleep and take care not to wake your bother." He released her hands and watched her go behind the tent's partition to her sleeping area.

She reminded him so much of her parents. Sadness filled

his heart as he recalled their death from a shadow hound attack in one of the camps. The shadow hounds had become fiercer in the past few years. Game in the mountainous region was scarce and the packs targeted the people's livestock. He shook his head. It was none of his concern, tomorrow he would take Keyla back to the city to live and train in peace. The other elders will return to the encampments of their clans. Laying down on his bedroll, his thoughts slowed as he descended into sleep.

* * *

"Again!" Keyla heard Myrron demand from the bench in the courtyard. Keyla focused her attention on her opponent. She looked in to her brother's eyes, trying to predict his next move. The summer sun blazed overhead as sweat trickled down her back under the thick layers of leather armor. The hilt of her sword was slick in her hand but she dare not slacken her grip. Wisps of black hair had escaped from the long braid that fell to her waist and fell about her face.

Slowly she circled the small courtyard of Myrron's home. The grass lawn had long since given way to a practice area for Keyla to learn her warrior skills. The past year had been grueling for Keyla both physically and mentally. Myrron stayed true to his word and had taught her all things that a shaman would need to know. Along with learning languages and history, she learned how to fight. Normally an apprentice of the shaman order would have many years of learning from a mentor. Keyla knew she did not have the luxury of time, and she studied from morning to dusk.

Keyla feinted and parried Syon's advances, trying to find a weakness she could exploit. Her brother had also learned from Myrron's warrior lessons and pressed her back. Feinting to her left, she twisted to the side and smacked her brother on his right arm with the flat of her blade. Cursing, Syon stepped back and deflected her second blow with his shield.

Keyla froze as a loud, demanding knock echoed from the front of Myrron's house. With a quick look at Myrron, she crossed to the other side of the courtyard to her traditional robes and slipped them over her leather armor, its multiple layers hiding the armors bulk. Her nose twitched at the smell of her armor; hopefully the guests would not get close enough to notice the smell of the sweat-drenched leather. She sheathed the sword and hid it in her robes. Calmly, she took a seat at the far end of the courtyard on one of the ornate benches as Myrron and Syon went into the house to answer the door.

Keyla heard shouts and the sound of something breaking inside the house. She rose to her feet, talking a few steps toward the screened panel that separated the house's interior from the courtyard. She jumped back as Syon came hurtling through it. He lay stunned and unmoving in the dirt of the practice yard, blood dripping from a wound over his eye. Four men came into the courtyard, and two of them held Myrron by the arms. Keyla stood still, conscious of keeping her armor from showing. She wondered briefly if they could hear her heart racing in her chest as she tried to retain an outward calm appearance.

She saw Myrron's head loll to the side, exposing red mark along his jaw, already turning into a bruise. Her eyes narrowed. *Who are these people to treat a councilor so roughly!* she thought, the white hot flame of anger began burning through her veins. Slowly, she eased her hand inside her robe, ready to grab her sword.

"Who are you? What do you want?" Keyla demanded, her voice unwavering.

One of the men stepped forward. "We are from the High

Council. We are here to take Councilor Myrron and his charges to face a tribunal for laws that have been broken. You will come with us."

"Keyla," Myrron groaned his voice barely a whisper, "go with them." He grimaced with pain and slumped unconscious.

Keyla stood indecisive for a moment, weighing her options. There were four large men and probably more outside. She frowned. It would be impossible to break through them without someone getting hurt or killed. She folded her hands in front of her, holding head high, she said. "I will go with you, if you do not hurt my family."

The men smiled at Keyla and one of them chuckled. "Come with us quietly and you won't be hurt. These one," he pushed Syon with his boot, turning him over, "tried to interfere and Elder Myrron stepped in at the wrong moment."

He looked chagrined. Even men like these knew better than to purposefully hurt an elder, at least Keyla hoped they wouldn't hurt him more. Still, she hesitated until the decision was taken from her.

The other man stepped forward and grabbed her painfully by the arm, pushing her roughly through Myrron's house to the front street. With little prompting, Keyla climbed into the covered carriage awaiting them. She released a soft sigh as they placed Myrron and Syon in the carriage with her and barred the door.

Tearing a length of cloth from her inner robe, Keyla quickly ministered aid Syon's and Myrron's injuries. She made a vexed sound as her anger grew at such rough treatment of her family.

"Keyla," Myrron said soothingly, rousing as she attended him, "try to calm yourself. You knew this day was a possibility."

"I know, but to see you treated so roughly makes me angry." Keyla paused in her ministrations as Myrron gripped her hand.

"If I remember correctly, it was I who decided to teach you." Myrron patted her hand. "Now don't worry too much. Let us hear what the high council has to say."

Keyla looked worriedly at her brother. Syon was still unconscious from the blow to his head. She leaned over and tucked back an errant strand of hair. He looked so young for his 17 years. Ever since their parent's death, he had tried to look after her and protect her. She knew once they were before the high council, Syon would try to defend her. She hoped he would awaken soon, so she could dissuade him from causing more trouble. He had a good heart, but she wished that he would use his head more often instead of brute force.

Keyla leaned back in her seat. Closing her eyes and focusing inward, she practiced the calming exercises Myrron had taught her years ago. Taking a deep breath, she exhaled slowly. She strove to calm the raging storm of her thoughts. Feeding them into a single flame until all the chaos was burned away. Now only her and the flame remained.

She opened her eyes as the carriage came to a halt outside the Council Hall, the largest building in Shilrey. It always amazed her that the ancestors had built such an impressive structure. Massive columns held up a peaked roof. Ornate carvings covered all surfaces, creating a dance of interweaving colors. Broad inlayed paving stones bordered the building. Plantings of innumerable flowers spread between the columns and the paved pathways. Normally this view gave her immense joy, now it only emanated a sense of foreboding.

The carriage door was unbarred and opened. The four men helped Myrron and Keyla down with more deference now that they were in view of the hall. She stood close to Myrron and felt a soft squeeze of encouragement as she gripped his wrinkled hand. Two of the men lifted Syon from the carriage and carried him to the hall. Myrron and Keyla followed with the other two men behind them.

Passing through the ornate metal doors, Keyla nearly halted in awe as she viewed the exquisite workmanship of the interior of the hall. From the stone floor to the tiled domed ceiling the ancient language of her people was carved upon the sand colored walls. Tall columns supported the archways along the corridors. Light streaked through the air from small openings set high into the outer wall. A small tug of her hand brought Keyla's attention back to Myrron. He gave her a gentle smile of understanding. She remembered that Myrron had seen the hall many times in his years as shaman and councilor. With hope, she didn't want her first time to walk these corridors to be her last.

They were led through the maze of corridors to an inner chamber. Once the two men deposited Syon in the room, Keyla and Myrron were left alone to attend to him.

"Keyla, dip a cloth into the water and bring to me." Myrron ordered her, sitting on a cushion next to Syon. "I will attempt to wake Syon and heal his wound."

Keyla quickly did as she was told and kneeled on the other side of Syon. Rarely has she had the chance to view the shaman's powers.

"This would work much better if I had my herbs," Myrron mumbled to himself.

Keyla studied Myrron. He removed the blood soaked bandage from Syon's head and replaced it with the damp cloth. His voice lifted in a chant that she had long since learned from his teachings. Lifting her head, she met Myrron's eyes.

A green fire flashed alive in his eyes, seeming to bore into her soul. Unbidden, she joined in the chant her softness in melody with his powerful voice.

Syon shifted and groaned under Myrron's hand. When his eyes opened wide, the chanting stopped, leaving behind nothing but the sound of Syon's exhaling breath.

Myrron was not looking at Syon instead his eyes were still locked with Keyla's. Slowly the green fire left his, eyes and a grin spread across his face. "You are strong my child even without her touch," Myrron assured her softly. Looking down at Syon, he removed the wet cloth from Syon's forehead, wiping off the rest of the blood that remained on his now unmarred skin.

"Where am I?" Syon rasped, his breath coming in shallow pants.

"Be still, Syon." Myrron placed a hand on his chest, preventing him from sitting up. "You received a good strike to the head and with your sister's help, you have been completely healed. It will take a little time for you to recover your strength."

"My help?" Keyla squeaked, startled.

"Yes, child." Myrron reached for her hand. "You have inadvertently passed one of the tests to be initiated in the order, the test to see if you can link to a shaman when performing a simple chant. Having you join me without any preparation is extraordinary and also proves that I am correct about you. You have amazing strength. Now," he broke his contact from Keyla, "help an old man to his feet, so we can discuss the tribunal."

"What about my armor?" Keyla asked, helping him to stand.

"I'm not sure you should take it off." Myrron looked at

her thoughtfully. "Something tells me that you may need it before the end."

"Need it?" Keyla questioned. "I am not going to threaten the councilors, am I?"

"No, nothing as severe as you might think. Enter the tribunal as you are dressed and keep in mind my teachings. This is a much larger test than you realize," he stated cryptically. "Now listen carefully, I fear we are running out of time."

While listening to the details Myrron recited, Keyla watched him pacing the small room. Worry began to twist her stomach. In the next few hours, the council will gather in the great hall and the tribunal will begin and sentence her fate and the fate of her family. She gathered her strength and courage. No matter the out come, she would see it through.

* * *

"Elder Myrron, Keyla and Syon, you have been summoned to a tribunal before the High Council of Shilrey. You have broken our laws that state you can not initiate a person in to the Order of the Shaman without approval from the council." Elder Yumma spoke from the dais before the prisoners. His withered hands folded on his staff as he leaned on it for support. The bright red of his council robes accented his pale, weathered features. "Make your statements to the tribunal."

Myrron walked to the middle of the floor. "I have trained her in the order," he began, an audible gasp was heard from the councilors. "She has the true gift and I have taught her accordingly. If she was born a boy, there would be no contestation."

Murmurs erupted in the hall. Elder Tarn stood and addressed Myrron, "You have confessed your crimes willingly and without coercion. You have also been touched, and, therefore, cannot lie." Tarn's lips tightened in a grimace, there was no precedence for these proceedings. "Elder Myrron, your title and property will be held in forfeit and you will be now known as Shaman Myrron. Another shaman shall be appointed as elder and will take over your duties to the city of Shilrey. Until such time the elders see that there will be no further threat from you to our society, you are here by restricted to the Hall. A room will be prepared for your residence."

"Myrron!" Keyla took a step forward when Myrron turned to leave and follow the guards out of the hall.

"You will be fine, child," Myrron soothed. "You knew this might happen. Remember what I have taught you, and you will be fine."

"Silence!" Elder Haim motioned for the guards to remove Myrron.

Keyla held her tongue as she waited for her judgment. In her mind, she attempted to achieve a calm state by feeding the flame her chaotic thoughts.

Tarn turned his attention to the two youths in front of him. "Keyla and Syon," he continued, "you will be sent to separate camps until you become of age. Then you can decide for yourself your residence. You will have no contact with Shaman Myrron."

"You can't separate us!" Syon yelled, stepping forward his fists clenched at his sides.

"Syon, you will address the council members appropriately," Elder Hiam admonished him. "I can see Myrron has had more of an influence on you than we suspected."

Keyla watched in shock as Syon rushed one of the guards.

"Keyla run!" he shouted, as he attempted to knock down the guard and take his weapon.

"Syon stop!" she commanded him, taking a step towards her brother and reaching out a hand to halt him.

The guard sidestepped Syon and captured his arm. He pinned Syon's arm behind his back and swung him around. He crossed his arm around Syon's chest, trapping him with his back to the guard.

"You will not go easily, child," he said, his muscles bulging as Syon struggled. The guard drew his blade and pressed it to Syon's throat. Syon looked over at Keyla, his eyes wide with fear.

Keyla swiftly reacted to the danger her brother was in. She drew her sword with a metallic rasp and strode towards the guard purposely. The Hall became deathly still.

"You dare bring a weapon to the tribunal!" Tarn shouted outraged.

An icy calm descended over Keyla, she held her blade steady to the guard holding her brother. "I do not want to harm anyone," her voice resonated throughout the hall. "Please, let my brother go."

"You have no choice in the matter, girl. Lower your weapon," Haim demanded from his council seat. "Do not make your situation worse."

"Elder Haim," Keyla turned her eyes upon him, her voice rough with emotion, "how worse could your decision be? You have taken Myrron from me. He has become my father these past years. Now, you are taking the last of my family, my brother, away. If that is your final judgment, then kill me now, for it will surely break my heart and I will die in the end."

Yumma's eyes briefly flared green. "She speaks the truth," he said suddenly.

"Elder Yumma?" Tarn looked at him in surprise. "This is merely a trick played to lessen her sentence."

"No, Elder Tarn. I believe she speaks the truth," he

repeated. "I knew her parents and out of consideration for them, perhaps a different solution could be arranged."

Keyla looked between Yumma and the guard. Hope budded in her breast. With a voice no less soft, she asked, "What solution do you propose, Elder Yumma?"

The councilors looked on with great interest as Yumma stepped down from his seat and crossed the floor to Keyla, the thump of his staff echoing in the vaulted hall. His green eyes contained a soft flame as he held her gaze. With a barely audible *hrumpf,* he reached for her sword and gently took it from her hands. Keyla's hands trembled and she folded them in front of her. She waited judgment for her foolish act.

Yumma turned to address the councilors, "Keyla is young. Elder Myrron has swayed her mind and tainted it with his foolishness. I propose both of these children be assigned to my camp in the mountains, and receive proper training to their station."

Keyla held her breath. *Where they really going to allow Syon and I to stay together?* She could hear the murmurs as the council members discussed Yumma's proposal. Her heart beat rapidly and a thousand butterflies made a home in her stomach. The calm she had a moment ago was shattered.

Tarn stood to address her, "It is agreed. Elder Yumma will be guardian of Keyla and Syon and take them to Meska camp. They will have no contact with Shaman Myrron until both Keyla and Syon become of age and are of their own mind. This is the decision of the High Council of Shilrey."

A small gasp was heard from Yumma. Keyla smiled, he did not anticipate becoming guardian of them. She looked at the guard still holding her brother with a blade to his throat. She gently placed a hand on Yumma's robe to get his attention. "Elder Yumma, could you have the guard remove his blade?"

Elder Yumma gave a start. "Yes, yes, of course, child." He motioned to the guard, "Release him."

Keyla saw her brother stumble as the guard released him. Syon turned to confront the guard, his posture rigid with anger. Before Syon could get them in more trouble, Keyla crossed the hall to him and hugged him close. "Don't Syon," she whispered in his ear. "We are safe. Let's go." She released him and waited for him to calm down.

"If there are no other objections to the sentencing of these two people," Tarn paused, briefly looking around the councilors, "then I call the tribunal of the High Council of Shilrey concluded."

* * *

Keyla was jarred awake as the carriage lurched, hitting another rut in the trail. Shifting on the pillows, she tried to find a more comfortable seat. Waiving the dust from her eyes, she looked through the opening in the covered carriage. Wind swept the long grass under the late afternoon sun, and the mountains loomed high above the flat plain. They traveled three days from the city and by nightfall, they would arrive at the mountain camp, Meska, and their new home. She could hear Syon talking with Yumma at the front of the cart. Their words were too soft to hear above the rumble of the carriage wheels and the horse and men riding along side the carriage.

A little knot of fear and worry had grown in her stomach, twisting painfully the closer they came to the mountains. She did not know what to expect when meeting the rest of the clansmen and wondered if they would accept her, since she knew so little about the clan's daily life.

Struggling through her memories, she tried to piece together what she remembered before her parents were killed. Vaguely, she could recall laughing with the other girls in a tent, playing a game and holding a rag doll. Keyla smiled at the happy memory. Unbidden the sight of her parents' mutilated bodies forced its way to the surface; she gasped and ruthlessly pushed the memory down. Panting slightly, a tear traced a path down her cheek through the dust. Another memory of Keyla and her mother at the riverside washing laundry singing a song together as they worked made her grin.

Keyla watched as the sky turned dark and stars appeared overhead. The first moon lay cradled between two of the mountain peeks. Scattered campfires glowed at the base of the mountain, marking the shepard's fields. Above the fires, a soft glow of the hundreds of campfires illuminated the true camp of the Meska Clan. The camp resided across a wide plateau a short ways up the cliff face that rose high above their heads to disappear in the night sky.

The carriage rumbled to a stop a short distance from a path that led up to the camp. The beasts would not be able to traverse its narrow, winding path with the carriage. Kayla stepped from the carriage looking for Yumma or Syon. Catching sight of them just stepping up the path, she quickly fell in behind them. Yumma looked behind him and gave her a small encouraging smile.

As they crested the top of the path, the plateau was spread out before them. The number of people who welcomed them home overwhelmed Keyla. She tried to put on a brave face and smiled at those who greeted her and her brother, but she also noticed that many of the clansmen frowned at her. She assumed word had come ahead of them that the girl who thought she was going to be a shaman was here. Lost in thought, she did not hear one of the older women trying to get her attention. With a soft tap on her arm, Keyla turned to see a woman holding a small pail of water and a towel.

"Keyla?" the woman asked, gesturing for her to follow. "Come with me."

She led Keyla to a large tent that had many colorful decorative symbols painted on the canvas. Once inside, Keyla stood nervously, not knowing what to expect.

"Keyla," the woman addressed her again, "My name is Sharri. I am kinswoman to Yumma and will be helping you adjust to your new home and the ways of the camp."

"N-nice to meet you, Sharri," Keyla stuttered in her nervousness.

Sharri paused shaking out the fresh robes from Keyla's trunk. She looked at Keyla with motherly warmth in her eyes. "You do not need to be nervous around us, Keyla. We know that what has happened to you is not your fault and I'll make sure that the clansmen know this."

"Yumma has told you about me?" Keyla was surprised that Yumma would have time so soon upon arriving.

"Yes." Sharri placed Keyla's robes on a low table. "He sent a letter ahead of the caravan to see that things were set in order for you and your brother's arrival. Come now and change. I'll help you wash your hair and then I will take you to Yumma's tent for something to eat."

Keyla did as Sharri told her and divested herself of her dirty traveling robes. After quickly washing, she dressed in a thin tunic. Sitting down on a cushion with her back facing a low table with a basin of water, she allowed Sharri to wash her hair. She shivered as the cold mountain water was poured over her scalp.

Sharri kept up a light chatter about what was to be expected of her in the next few weeks.

How Keyla was going to learn everything in only a few

weeks, she did not know. Other girls would have been taught these things from the time they became a young woman. Keyla did not have the chance to learn from her mother or another woman. Myrron had a couple of people from the city come in and do the cleaning for him. Keyla and Syon spent most of the years living with Myrron reading and learning books and histories, then this last year learning the old language, chants and lore. Keyla sighed as Sharri rubbed her hair with a towel.

"Are you tired?" Sharri asked, misinterpreting her sigh. "I am not surprised after three days traveling that rough road. Come and get into the rest of your clothes and I'll take you to Yumma's tent."

Keyla didn't want to explain to Sharri what she was thinking and dressed silently. She liked Sharri with her warmth and affection, accepting her without judgment.

Maybe others will do the same, she thought. A hope blossomed that perhaps things would turn out well here. It was a small hope.

Keyla heard murmurs of other conversations floating with the breeze coming down from the mountain. Occasionally, she could hear her name or Syon's name but she could not figure out what they were saying. Keyla recited a calming chant in her head, one that Myrron had taught her when they first began her training. She knew better than to say the words out loud but took comfort in the fact that even though Myrron was no longer there his words were with her.

A small smile graced her face as she greeted Yumma and entered her new home.

* * *

Keyla eased the buckets to the ground and lifted the yoke off her shoulders. She smiled to herself. It was the first time she carried the water up the canyon trail to the camp without stopping. She knew she was much stronger than when she arrived at the camp six months ago. She stretched, arching her back. Lifting the yoke back on her shoulders, she made her way through the camp to Yumma's tent.

Placing the buckets inside the tent, she turned to find Yumma smiling at her. Keyla grinned in return. "Good day, Elder Yumma," Keyla welcomed him.

"Girl, I have told you before that you may call me Yumma in the camp," he admonished her.

"Yes, Yumma, you have told me many times." Keyla's grin widened when she noticed the bundle Yumma was carrying.

"Ah," he gave her the bundle, "as you know there is a marriage ceremony tonight, and I want you to be present."

Keyla looked up at him sharply, "Yumma, they don't accept me here, not everyone. To them, I am a disgrace to the clan."

"That is because they do not know you, my dear. You have shown great efforts in starting a new life here and forgetting your past. Yet, you hide away from everyone except Sharri and myself." Yumma tapped the bundle with his knobby finger. "It is a gift from Sharri and I want you to wear it tonight."

Keyla looked down at the bundle with a tear in her eye. They have done so much for her. She looked up at him and with weariness of heart, she agreed, "Yes Yumma."

"Good girl, now go get ready. I have things I must attend to this afternoon, then I will be back in time to escort you to the ceremony." Yumma pushed back the tent flap with his staff and hobbled down the well-worn path between the tents.

After closing the tent flap, Keyla sat on a cushion and

untied the bundle. Shaking out the material, she lifted it before her eyes. Layers of near-translucent, soft, white cloth cascaded down to the floor. Small blue flowers and vines were embroidered around the neckline and hemline. The waist was tied with a wide blue ribbon. It was the finest robe she had ever seen. A piece of metal fell from the folds of the cloth. Setting the robe carefully to the side, she picked up the metal. Turning it over in her hand, it was a hairpiece that looked like two joined butterflies set in silver.

Tears fell gently into her hands. She didn't deserve this. Every night, before going to sleep, she went through the rituals Myrron had taught her, reciting mentally his teachings and chants least she forget. Despair settled upon her heart. Her brother had fallen in love with one of the shepherd's daughters and had less time for Keyla. Syon was accepted by the other hunters and shepherds of the camp. Even now, he was in the lower plain protecting the herds.

Keyla laid the hairpiece on the robe. Taking one of the buckets to the low table on the far side of the tent, she poured out a generous amount into a bowl. If Yumma wanted her to appear tonight, she was going to look her best. Taking the braid out of her hair, she began washing it.

Long shadows played upon the sides of the tent when Yumma came for her. Keyla stood, smoothing out the folds of the robe and checking to make sure her hair was still secured in the butterfly piece at the nape of her neck. She tucked errant strands of hair behind her ears. She smiled faintly at Yumma's proud grin.

"Come. It is time to go." Yumma motioned her to follow him.

She could hear near by music already entertaining the clansmen gathered for the ceremony. It was a short walk to the center of the camp. Long trestle tables and benches had been set up along the perimeter of the clearing. The colorful clothing of the clansmen added to the merriment of the occasion. Keyla couldn't help but smile as children raced around, holding short poles with long ribbons tied to the ends.

She sat at the far end of Yumma's table, knowing many people would come to greet the Elder. She was not disappointed, and soon the table filled with adults talking with Yumma. A few of them sat and chatted with Keyla, complimenting her on her new robe.

"Ah," Sharri grinned as she sat next to Keyla, "I told Yumma that you would look radiant in this color. It took me a better part of the past moon phase to embroider your robe. I think that is something I will need to teach you next."

Keyla ducked her head in embarrassment, she was not used to such compliments from so many people.

Shortly the music stopped, and a lone drummer beat a slow march, indicating the start of the ceremony. Keyla stood with the other people at her table as the couple walked to the center of the green. Yumma followed them in his bright red ceremonial robes. The couple turned to face Yumma and kneeled on two cushions placed before them. Soft chanting, lifted up in candence, joined Yumma's voice in the song of marriage.

When the chanting stopped, Keyla sniffled with a tear in her eye. Moved with the beauty of the moment, she thought perhaps someday she too would be standing in front of the elder to be joined with the one she loved. She smiled to herself. It was a lovely dream.

As the second moon was rising, Keyla found herself alone at the table. Yumma had already retired to their tent for the evening. Keyla played with the ends of a ribbon, enjoying the music and watching the people dance. A large shadow loomed over her, blocking the light from the torches. Startled, she looked up and found Durnal, one of the newly appointed shepherds, looking down at her with a smile. His shorn hair stuck up in places and his eyes shown with mischief.

Durnal held out his hand. "Care for a dance?"

With a shy smile, Keyla placed her hand in his. The tempo of the music changed to a fast rhythm, the drums setting the pace and the windpipes following merrily. A ring of dancers formed with a second inner circle. Durnal led Keyla to the edge of the outer circle and with a tug on her hand she found herself swept away, laughing. She smiled as the tempo changed and the circles broke to long lines snaking between tents and tables. Coming together once again, the circles surrounded the newly married couple. Keyla joined in the song of love and loyalty.

When the song ended, Keyla clapped and cheered with the rest of the clan members. Hope filled her heart that she now belonged. She felt Durnal take her hand once more. She turned to face him as the music fell in a slow beat. With his arms around her, she wished the night would last forever. She tilted her head, looking into his warm eyes. He smiled down at her. Her heart fluttered madly in her chest as he slowly bent down and kissed her. She barely felt his lips brush hers. As he turned his head to hold her close his breath was a warm caress on her cheek.

A harsh scream shattered the night. Shouts were heard near the cliff wall. The music stopped, and the celebrants scattered to see what the commotion was about. A lone howl cut through the night air, rooting Keyla to the middle of the courtyard as Durnal dashed away. More howls joined the first, promising death under the moon lit sky. Keyla stumbled as someone knocked into her. Recovering her balance, she turned on her heel and raced to her tent.

Keyla threw back the flap of the tent, coming face to face with Yumma. "Where are they?" she demanded.

"What are you talking about?" Yumma asked, frowning at her.

"My armor, my sword, I know you still poses them." Keyla stated, with all deference aside, looking wildly around the tent.

Yumma drew himself up in front of her. "That time for you has passed." He held up a hand when he saw she was going to argue with him. "I don't have time for this right now. You will remain in the tent until after the shadow hounds are dealt with. This isn't the first time shadow hounds raided our camp, and it won't be the last. Stay here," he ordered. Taking his healer's satchel with him, Yumma left Keyla alone and fuming in the tent.

With a grumble, that could have rivaled one the shadow hound's growls, Keyla crossed the tent. As gently as her hurried state would allow, she started searching through Yumma's things looking for the armor that Myrron had given her. Her anxiety rose, Syon was out there, and from what she heard there were at least twenty of the beasts descended upon the lower plain. A small cry escaped her throat when she opened a long chest. There, nestled in layers of rugs, was her armor and sword.

A sense of urgency filled Keyla's heart as she changed, her fingers swiftly buckling the armor in place. She lifted her sword before her, the sheath and baldric forgotten on the floor of the tent. Moments later, passing the startled gasps of the clansmen, she ran down the canyon path to the lower plains, towards the beasts that had killed her parents and towards her brother.

Thunder crashed, announcing the swiftly approaching

storm. Clouds rolled overhead, hiding the moon in its folds. Wind howled, momentarily drowning out the sounds of the beasts and men. The long grass of the field bent like land locked waves of water. The deluge of rain poured from the clouds, biting into those below.

The metallic smell of blood invaded her senses. Scattered torches from the shepherds' outpost illuminated the colorless landscape in their flickering light. Part of Keyla, that was still the young girl, shrank from the nightmarish scene before her; the other part, conditioned from Myrron's training in the order, calmly surveyed the battle between beast and man. The shadow hounds cornered animal and man alike, stalking, circling and snarling their bestial growls. One by one she could see her clansmen and animals fell, torn limb from limb by the beasts. The animals screamed in terror, milling about the plain. They tried bolting, only to find their path blocked by more shadow hounds.

Syon was pressed against the far canyon, holding off three of the beasts. With a battle cry, from the ancient language of her people, she surged forward across the plain. Halfway to her brother's side, she saw one of the shadow hounds. It lifted its bloody muzzle from an animal carcass and turned towards her. She slowed to a stop, waiting for the beast to advance. Her fear was forgotten.

The shadow hound snarled, revealing yellow fangs. Its ears lay back against its immense head. The fall of the rain didn't reduce the stench that permeated the air from its dark matted hair. Its yellow eyes glowed in the dieing firelight of the torches as it slowly crept closer to her. Keyla held her sword steady, briefly thinking that she had only been taught against humans not shadow hounds that were nearly as tall as she.

The beast lunged at her. Keyla twisted to the side, like

she had done so many times in Myrron's courtyard, and ducked under the mass of the shadow hound. She screamed with pain as the shadow hound's claws raked her shoulder. Tumbling to the ground, she rolled away from the beast. Regaining her feet, she rose with new determination. The beast would not take her this night.

Her leather armor had protected her from the claws, the scratches where shallow and did not impede her movement. Easing her shoulders, she followed the movements of the circling beast. Not taking her gaze from the shadow hound, she realized another warrior had joined her. From the corner of her eye, she recognized Durnal.

"You shouldn't be here!" he shouted over the thunder.

Keyla ignored him as the beast lunged toward Durnal. Quickly, she stepped to the side and with both hands on the hilt of her sword stabbed the beast in the side and through its heart. Shock from the impact traveled up her arms as the sword was torn from her hands. The beast fell to the thickening mud, its dark blood joining those of his brethren as his breath stilled.

Durnal stood over the beast, his left arm bloodied with claw marks, and his right hand still holding his sword. His disbelief and awe showed plainly on his face.

With a nod and a small smile to Durnal, she placed her foot on the carcass and pulled free her sword. Keyla turned her attention back to her brother and saw that he had killed two of the beasts. Pride swelled in her breast, but it was not over yet. Another one of the dreadful beasts still remained, pressing Syon back against the canyon wall. It was larger than most, nearly as tall as Syon. Its black matted fur stood out in stark contrast to the pale grey canyon stone. Syon also seemed to be favoring his sword arm. Keyla's eyes narrowed in the few brief moments it took to assess the situation. Her brother was hurt and needed her help. Not acknowledging Durnal's startled shout, Keyla raced over the sodden plain as lightning forked through the sky.

Nearing her brother, she watched in horror as the beast bit into Syon's shoulder. His anguished scream carried over the din of the battle. With one last thrust, Syon embedded his sword in the beast killing it, both beast and man falling to the ground.

Keyla rushed to her brother's side, kneeling with a small splash in the mud and rain. In death, the shadow hound had loosened its jaw and fell atop Syon, trapping him. Renewed anger gave strength to Keyla, allowing her to shove the heavy carcass off her brother.

She gently removed her brother's wrecked armor. Gasping at the sight of the ragged wounds, Keyla quickly tore strips of Syon's tunic and wrapped his wounds securely, stanching the flow of blood.

"Syon! Syon!" she shouted at him, tears streaming down her face. "Don't you dare die on me now. Stay with me." Keyla continued talking to him as she held her brother close. Syon's chest rose and fell as he struggled with each rasping breath. She knew he would not live long if she couldn't get him to a shaman soon. She looked around desperately but the other warriors were too far to hear her shout. None of the remaining shadow beasts had noticed them beside the canyon wall.

"Syon no. Don't give up," Keyla fervently pleaded, her heart thudding painfully in her chest.

Syon's breath became shallow. His skin grew colder as the icy rain washed the blood from his skin.

Desperation and fear bloomed inside her, a catalyst to

the anger that threatened to engulf her. Memories of her parents lying on the ground, much like Syon, forced their way through Keyla's mind. The clansmen had found her sobbing over their bloodied bodies. Keyla started trembling, she didn't want Syon to join them. She didn't want to be left alone. She tilted back her head and screamed to the heavens, her tears mingling with the rain.

An eerie call of a thousand birds in one voice answered Keyla's cry. Piercing the darkened clouds, The One Dragon came. Her long serpent body was covered with glittering opal scales, reflecting the forked lighting of the storm in a multitude of colors. Short forelegs and powerful hind legs were stretched back in flight as translucent wings carried the magnificent creature effortlessly on the currents of air. Another voice of song filled the air as the winged beast swooped over the battle, hunting the beasts down and dispatching them. Shadow hounds howled in defiance before scattering to the mountain pass at the far end of the small canyon. The One Dragon circled once more over the field. The few remaining warriors and the clansmen from the camp could be heard cheering in victory.

Cold draughts of air wafted about her, plastering her wet hair to her face. Shivering in her sodden leather armor, she looked into large emerald eyes that swirled with a mystical flame. The One Dragon settled on her haunches before Keyla.

Child, why have you not come before me? She inquired of Keyla, in a voice that was not a voice but rather impressions in her mind.

"I was not permitted great one." Keyla softly replied. A soft warmth enveloped her. Keyla knew that she was safe and nothing more was going to harm her or her brother. With a long look at her brother, she gently laid him on the ground. Keyla emptied her mind of all thought and emotion until only the flame remained, instinctively following what she was taught by Myrron so long ago in preparation for when she would meet the dragon.

Come, kneel before me. You have the strongest gift I have seen in moons beyond count. The great dragon lowered her head level with Keyla's kneeling form. *Long have the prophecies have told of you. You shall be the first woman who holds the power since your ancestors fled their homeland. Now clear you mind, child, and don't fight me. Let your mind become one with mine.*

Keyla whimpered with the onslaught of the touch. Shivers wracked her body as a green glow surrounded her. Knowledge beyond infinite encompassed her mind, delving, and expanding until Keyla became one with the dragon.

Where am I? Keyla wondered, seeing nothing beyond a green light.

You are with me, child. It is good you have reached the first stage. I have given you the knowledge of your elders. Keyla sensed pleasure coming from the dragon. *You are truly strong to have reached this place so quickly.*

What is this place?

It exists out of time, and out of place. It is nothing and everything, the dragon cryptically replied. *It is time for you to take the next step. The step all those before you have taken to become shaman. Remember who you are.*

Keyla arched her back as a scream tore from her throat. Pain of a hundred daggers struck her mind, obliterating all other senses. Agony burned through her veins, slowly incinerating her in its fiery inferno. Vaguely, she could hear the song of a thousand birds join her screams as the dragon voiced her song. Moments passed, long in her head but short in time. Keyla became silent as the pain receded into a warm embrace, and the power of the shamans filled her.

Child? The dragon's voice permeated her senses.

"I am here," Keyla said faintly. Looking around, she found herself gently cradled in one of the dragon's claws.

You have done well, Shaman Keyla. You will walk among the Shilrey as a healer and a leader. The One Dragon's eyes shown with the fiery green flames of power as she regarded Keyla.

Overcome with emotion, Keyla stretched her arm to Syon. "Help him," she pleaded softly.

Keyla watched as she picked up Syon with her other claw. Her mind was still dazed from the onslaught of the touch. With a small lurch, The One Dragon took to the air, quickly gliding over the lower plain. Keyla closed her eyes against the sight of all the dead torn and bloody on the field below. Too few remaining warriors were walking towards the camp.

She felt hands lifting her from the dragon's grasp and placing her on a soft rug. The song of the dragon vibrated through her as The One Dragon launched to the sky. Opening her eyes, she saw many of the clansmen above her. She heard startled gasps and shouts for Yumma.

Why would they call Yumma? Keyla thought sleepily. *I'm so tired.*

A sharp pain flared across her cheek, then again on her other cheek. Raising her hand, she tried to ward off the blows. Dimly, she heard someone saying her name. She wished they would talk louder so she could hear them.

"Keyla!" Yumma called to her, concern saturating his voice.

"Yes," she answered groggily.

"Open your eyes, Keyla."

Keyla tried hard to open her eyes. It was very difficult. Slowly, she forced them open and stared in to Yumma's bright green eyes hovering bare inches from her face.

"You've been touched."

"Syon," Keyla forced the words out of her roughened throat, "is he alive?"

"Yes Keyla." Yumma tucked her hair behind her ear. "Syon is alive. I have healed his severest injuries. Drink this," he held a cup of herbal potion to her lips, "and sleep."

* * *

Keyla walked with Yumma between the tents to the councilors meeting. Nerves fluttered in her stomach. Though, she knew they could not deny her the position of Shaman, she also knew she was not wanted among them.

"Yumma?" Keyla gained his attention. "I'm nervous. What if they don't accept me?"

His knowing eyes peered up at her from his winkled face. "Don't fret, child," Yumma admonished her. "You have been chosen despite tradition. We will train you to use the power you have received. You know this."

"Yumma," Keyla hesitated, "will I be able to request Myrron to be released and his property restored?"

Yumma's frowned thoughtfully, "He still broke the laws of the land by training you without the council's approval, but with light of what's happened there may be a change in his sentence." Yumma raised a hand to stop her from talking. "You will do best to be quiet and let me speak for you once in the tribunal."

"Yes Yumma," Keyla said, still feeling the youth trying to play an adult. She was grateful that Yumma would not allow Syon to join them. He was still healing from his injuries that Yumma did not have the strength to fully heal with his power. There had been too many warriors who required Yumma's power that night and it had drained him.

Yumma held back the flap for Keyla to enter the large common tent that was used for the councilors meeting today. Yumma settled himself at the far end of the tent, among the large cushions set for the elders. Keyla found herself looking at the circle of councilors much like she had many moons ago.

Elder Tarn led the councilors in the opening formalities and addressed Keyla, "Shaman Keyla, The One Dragon has singled you out to become shaman and is beyond contestation. You will be given the training your station merits."

"Be that as it may," Elder Haim interrupted. "Who's going to teach her? Certainly not I."

Keyla listened as each of the councilors declined to teach her. Her heart felt heavy in her chest. She has accomplished what Myrron had told her she would and yet, to have come so far, she was still just a girl to them.

Yumma regarded Keyla, his gaze revealing a slight twinkle. "If I may make a suggestion." Yumma stood, quieting the other councilors. "It would seem that there is only one person willing to continue Keyla's training in the order, and it be not I."

Keyla frowned in confusion, *If Yumma doesn't want me, then who could it be?*

Yumma raised a hand to once again silence the council members. "Shaman Myrron is the only one who would be willing to train Shaman Keyla in the duties that are required of the Order of the Shamans. In light of The One Dragon's choice, it would seem that Myrron had been correct in his assessment. I request he be released to my camp. Under my watchful eye, he shall train young Shaman Keyla in the order."

Discussions broke out amongst the councilors; many of the elders were clearly upset at the turn of events. Barely able to take a breath, Keyla grasped her hands in front of her to keep them from shaking. She heard her and Myrron's names, but could not hear what they were saying about them.

"Enough!" Elder Tarn stood, addressing the council. "If there is no good reason why we should not grant Elder Yumma's request, then I say let him have the trouble makers. I do not want to see either of them again until Shaman Keyla has completed her training."

Yumma nodded, thumping his cane on the carpeted ground for good measure.

Tarn surveyed the councilors. None returned his gaze. "Then it is done. Elder Yumma will retain guardianship over Shaman Keyla until she becomes of age. Shaman Myrron will be restricted to your camp and train Shaman Keyla in the order until such time that she is presented to the tribunal for her final tests."

Keyla jumped when someone touched her shoulder. Turning around, she stared in shock at the person behind her. Disregarding all sense of dignity, she flung her arms around him, causing a few raised eyebrows among the council members.

"Well," Myrron gruffly said, still engulfed in Keyla's hug, "you have done it, dear child. Though I cannot call you child anymore, can I, Shaman Keyla?"

"Not any more." Keyla replied, releasing him.

"Shaman Myrron," Tarn's voice interrupted them, "it is the decision of the Council that you are to remain here at Meska to train Keyla until such time she completes her tests to the order. Elder Yumma will supervise her training."

Keyla held tight to Myrron's hand. Her heart sung with joy, at long last she would begin her destiny in public with the council's approval.

"Shaman Keyla and Shaman Myrron, you may go now." Haim said from the shadowed corner of the tent.

Keyla glanced at him.

Haim smiled at her and motioned for them to go.

Stepping outside, she blinked in the bright sunlight and held the tent flap open for Myrron. She fell into step beside him as they walked toward Yumma's tent. Passing three women carrying baskets of wet clothes, Keyla stopped and turned.

"Excuse me," Keyla interrupted them. "I thought I heard my name called. Did you want to say something to me?"

The three women looked at her as if she had just crawled from the belly of a shadow hound. One of them stepped forward, ignoring Myrron, she addressed Keyla, "I have nothing to say to you. I do not know why The One Dragon chose such a worthless clansmen but I …"

"You will treat Shaman Keyla with the respect due her station." Myrron spoke sharply to the woman.

"Her station is undeserved," the woman replied just as sharply.

Keyla stepped in front of Myrron and stared at the woman. She felt a soft stirring of the power. "I am Shaman Keyla and this is Shaman Myrron. If you cannot," Keyla paused, taking a deep breath and her voice lowered, "or will not respect us as being among the chosen, then you will be quiet."

The other two women pulled her away from Keyla and Myrron whispering fiercely for her to remain quiet. With a glance back at them, the three women entered a nearby tent.

Keyla sighed.

"Keyla, the people do not know how to react to you," Myrron said, pulling her aside to walk between the tents out of view of the other clansmen. "Do not judge them to harshly. You are the first woman to be chosen by The One Dragon since the ancient time. That alone is enough for them to be confused and perhaps even a little frightened of you."

"Frightened of me?" Keyla asked him unbelievingly. "Did you hear what that woman said to me? It was insulting."

"Keyla, you must learn to have more patience," he said, stopping her. "They will need to learn to treat you according to your station. You must leave the child Keyla behind you and take on the role of Shaman Keyla. Despite your age, the clansmen are now your children and you have the power to protect them."

"I know." Keyla looked out over the plateau, the sun had begun setting behind the mountaintops. "It's just…I thought things would be different now."

"Different how?" Myrron inquired.

"I thought that I would be accepted by the clansmen because she chose me. I did not go looking for her, she found me that night and gave me this wonderful gift." Keyla locked eyes with Myrron as she drew on her power.

"Keyla," He said with a warning in his voice, "You don't have the training to draw this much power."

"I-I don't think I can stop," Keyla stuttered, the power continuing to surge into her. She turned and stumbled out from between the tents onto the common area. The same common area where she had followed her heart and had left the girl behind, going forth as a warrior to fight the shadow hounds that fated night. She stopped in the middle of the yard. She had never felt so alive, so connected to everything. She could feel the warmth of the sun-baked clay beneath her feet. Reaching out with her enhanced senses, she felt the life around her, in the insects and worms in the near by grass, and in the people and animals in the camp. She closed her eyes and tilted her head to the sky.

She soaked in the warmth of the last rays of the afternoon sunlight as it fell upon her face. It seemed to kindle a fire inside her, causing the power to rage, coursing through her veins and tingling her skin. Vaguely, she could hear people murmuring around her. They did not touch her, nor did she want to be touched right now. She opened her eyes to a world tinted with green flame.

She watched the Elders gather in a circle around her. Feeling a burning sensation in her hands, she lifted one before her eyes. A soft green glow surrounded her hand and slowly climbed up her arm. She started at it, utterly fascinated by the movement of her fingers; slowly, she focused on the people beyond her hand. The clansmen lined the common area and peered out from between the tents, and children wide-eyed and silent kneeled in front of their parents.

Low rhythmic chanting emerged from the circle of elders. It tried to sooth the fire within her, but the fire was not listening. The power was awakened. It needed to be used or it would incinerate her. The last rays of the sun fell behind the mountain, leaving Meska in twilight. Keyla sunk to one knee as the power became too much to bear.

The chanting rose in pitch and urgency. She felt a subtle probe of her mind as the elders were trying to reach her to drain her of her power. The power did not like that, and neither did she. Keyla placed both palms flat on the ground now cool without the sun warming its surface. She concentrated on her breathing and felt the probing once more.

They are not going to take it away from me. The power is mine! Keyla screamed inside her mind. The power rose to an inferno trying to burn all that was in its path. Keyla vaguely recalled feeling this rush of power inside her when The One Dragon had touched her. However, now she was alone to deal with the onslaught.

Keyla tried to pull her scattered thoughts together and concentrate on the power, molding it to do her bidding. With every heartbeat a measured time, the power bent to her will. She kept her eyes focused on the ground in front of her and her hands that glowed fiercely with green flame in the fading light.

With only one thought of water to quench the firestorm in her soul, she sent the power deep into the earth. The after-shock of the power sent a concussion radiating out from her, flattening people and tents in its force. Small tremors became larger tremors as the power dove, seeking water for its mistress. Keyla gripped the dirt in front of her, riding out the waves of power as they left her body. The ground tilted under Keyla's feet, throwing her on to her back, the last of the power spent.

"Keyla!" Durnal shouted, coming through the collapsed tents to kneel at her side. "Keyla," he repeated, gently taking her into his arms.

Keyla looked into Durnal's eyes. With clarity of those of the chosen, she saw his true devotion to her. He was not afraid of who she was or what she was. She gave him a small, tired smile. "I'm fine, just tired."

Durnal held Keyla close as a second powerful tremor shook the ground. A resounding crack was heard as the ground split where Keyla had sent the power. With a flash of green fire, a fountain of water shot into the air. The power did as she inadvertently requested, it retrieved water to quench the flames.

Laughing, she held out her hand to catch the spray as it fell, drenching both of them. Durnal shifted slightly, looking around. Keyla followed his gaze and noticed the devastation she had caused. Her laughter died in her throat as a choked sob left her lips. The elders were busy checking if anyone hurt and helping up those who have fallen. Unable to look any further, she buried her head in Durnal's shoulder and sobs racked her body as her emotions overwhelmed her.

"Keyla?" Myrron asked, concern coloring his voice. "Keyla, no one is hurt. Your power manifesting was normal. I just didn't expect it to come so soon." Myrron put a hand on her shoulder.

Looking up at her old friend, she let the falling water wash her tears away. With Durnal's help, she stood up on unsteady legs and leaned against him for support.

"Everything is going to be fine." Durnal assured her as he brushed back the wet strands of hair clinging to her cheek.

With his encouraging smile, she turned to face her people. She gazed at the fallen tents and saw that, indeed, no one was hurt. The Elders had put the clansmen to work and the tents were regaining their previous forms. Keyla noticed that the people paused from putting up the tents and looked at her. Their faces reflected fear and uncertainty.

"You are wrong," She disagreed softly. "Nothing is fine, nor will it be for a long time."

Myrron spoke from behind them, "I knew when I first saw your mind's strength that you were special. The One

Dragon gave you her gift of the power and at a strength that has not been seen since the ancient days. People will remember this day for many years to come. The day when Shaman Keyla, one of the chosen, a leader and a healer brought forth a new era for the people of Shilrey."

About The Authors

JoEllen Drazan is a writer and sometimes editor who lives in Minnesota, U.S.A. She has been a professional artist for 18 years and runs a web development business, Drazan Enterprises, at www.drazan.com and a writer's forum at www.drazan.us. Special thanks to fellow author Hannah Steenback, who helped when help was needed most.

Angie Mansfield lives right in the center of the U.S.A., where nothing interesting ever happens. So she has to make stuff up. With the help of lots of…umm, caffeine. Yeah, that's it. Caffeine…

Tracy Crowe is a career college student and enjoys writing, crocheting, and hanging out on the Soapbox. When she grows up she would like to be either a pirate or a university professor.

ChaosInOrder is, well, ChaosIn Order… :)

K.A. Thompson is a freelance writer and the author of three novels: *Charybdis*, *As Simple As That*, and *Finding Father Rabbit*. She has recently left Ohio and moved back to California with her husband of 23 years (affectionately known as The Spouse Thingy) following his joyous retirement from the U.S. Air Force (read: Yeehaw! A real paycheck now!) they have an adult son (Curt, look for him, he's an actor) and a psychotic cat named Max. Peek inside her head at kathompson.blogspot.com.

Special thanks to Tony Lee Healey, who gave the idea and title for this book, and to the readers and writers at the 'box.

"We've all come into contact with someone who has lost their life to Cancer, or suffered because of it, and it would be a good thing for the people of the 'box to do what they can and help fight it." – *Tony Lee Healey*

Sponsored by
Drazan Enterprise
Rochester, Minnesota USA
http://www.drazan.com